Thirty - Second Edition

THE 2010 CALIFORNIA NOTARY LAW PRIMER

*All the hard-to-find information
every California Notary Public
needs to know!*

National Notary Association

Published by:

National Notary Association
9350 De Soto Avenue,
Chatsworth, CA 91311-4926
(818) 739-4000
Fax: (818) 700-0920
www.NationalNotary.org
eMail: nna@nationalnotary.org

The information in this *Primer* is correct and current at the time
of its publication, although new laws, regulations and rulings
may subsequently affect the validity of certain sections. This
information is provided to aid comprehension of state Notary Public
requirements and should not be construed as legal advice. Please
consult an attorney for inquiries relating to legal matters.

Thirty-Second Edition © 2009
Second Printing (2010)
First Edition © 1978

ISBN No. 1-59767-064-2

SEHADA SAHMAXONE

Table
of Contents

Introduction

The National Notary Association commends you on your interest in California Notary law! Purchasing *The California Notary Law Primer* identifies you as a conscientious professional who takes your official duties seriously.

In few fields is the expression "more to it than meets the eye" truer than in Notary law. What often appears on the surface to be a simple procedure may, in fact, have important legal considerations.

The purpose of *The California Notary Law Primer* is to provide you with a resource to help decipher the many intricate laws that affect notarization. In so doing, the Primer will acquaint you with all of the important aspects of California's Notary law and with prudent notarial practices in general.

This edition of *The California Notary Law Primer* contains the law changes to the Civil Code made by Chapter 67 of the Laws of 2007 and effective January 1, 2009.

While *The California Notary Law Primer* begins with informative chapters on how to obtain your commission, what tools the Notary needs, often-asked questions and critical steps in notarization, the heart of this book is the chapter titled "Notary Laws Explained." Here, we take you through the myriad of Notary laws and put them in easy-to-understand terms. Every section of the law is analyzed and explained, as well as topics not covered by California law but nonetheless of vital concern to you as a Notary.

For handy reference, we have reprinted the pertinent sections of the state laws that relate to Notaries Public. In addition, we have included addresses and phone numbers of Secretary of State offices, county clerk offices and Bureaus of Vital Statistics, plus a list of nations that are parties to the Hague Convention, a treaty that simplifies the process of authentication.

Whether you are about to be commissioned for the first time, or a longtime Notary, we are sure that *The California Notary Law Primer* will provide you with new insight and understanding.

> Milton G. Valera
> President
> National Notary Association

How to Become a California Notary Public

1. Ensure that you comply with the basic qualifications for a California Notary commission.

First, you must be a legal resident of the state. Second, you must be 18 years of age or older. And third, you must not have been convicted of a felony or of a crime involving moral turpitude.

U.S. citizenship is not required as long as you legally reside in this country under federal law. There is no minimum time of state residency — you can apply for a commission on the same day that you enter California. A "legal resident" is a person who is residing in the state and who intends to stay, as indicated usually by taking action to obtain a driver's license, registering to vote or the like.*

2. Obtain a commission application and Notary exam registration instructions.

Whether you are applying for a Notary commission for the first time or you are renewing your commission, you must pass a written and proctored examination administered at designated sites throughout California.

To receive a commission application and instructions on registering for the exam, call Cooperative Personnel Services (CPS)** at (916) 263-3520, Monday through Saturday, 6 a.m. to 7 p.m. Exams are also offered following National Notary Association seminars. Call the NNA at (800) 876-6827 for

---

*California may also appoint Notaries to act only on a given U.S. military base. The applicant must be a U.S. citizen, a federal civil servant and recommended by the commanding officer of the base. Such four-year commissions terminate when employment on the base ends.

**Cooperative Personnel Services is a private firm, contracted by the Secretary of State to administer California's Notary Public exam at sites throughout the state.

information or to sign up for a seminar and exam. Usually you will receive an official Notary commission application, exam registration instructions, a list of exam dates and a California Notary Public Handbook within a week of calling CPS or the NNA.

To avoid a gap between commissions, renewing Notaries may begin the application process up to one year before their commissions expire.

3. Study the Notary Public Handbook.

The 30-question, multiple-choice exam is based upon the California Notary Public Handbook, which should be studied thoroughly. It is also helpful to review the "Notary Laws Explained" chapter of this Primer, starting on page 19.

4. Complete the application.

Follow the clear instructions on the reverse side of the application. Be aware that any false statements or omission of any information required by this form is cause for denial of a Notary commission.

5. Take the state-approved education course.

California law requires Notaries Public appointed on or after July 1, 2005, whether renewing or first time, to have completed an approved six-hour course covering a Notary's duties. Effective July 1, 2009, renewing Notaries who have completed a state-approved, six-hour course and whose commissions have not yet expired must complete a refresher course of at least three hours.

A list of authorized education providers is available on the Secretary of State's Web site at www.sos.ca.gov.

6. Register for the exam.

Select a convenient location and time, and register for the exam, following the instructions provided. You may register by mail at least 11 business days prior to the requested exam date, or by calling (916) 263-3520. You may also show up at an exam site without registering beforehand, but space may be limited.

A confirmation letter for the exam will be sent to you if your registration is received at least 11 business days prior to the exam date. To sign up for an NNA seminar and the subsequent state exam, call (800) 876-6827.

7. Take the exam.

Report to the selected site 60 minutes before the designated exam time. For walk-ins, the policy is first-come, first-served.

Be prepared to present:

- Identification — a state driver's license or nondriver's ID, U.S. or foreign passport, U.S. Military ID or Mexican or Canadian driver's license, provided it is current or has been issued within the last five years.

- Commission fee — a check or money order for $40 (payable to "Secretary of State") with your printed name and Social Security number written on the lower left side. Each applicant must have a separate check or money order. The $40 fee is for both new and renewing commission applicants. The fee for applicants retaking the exam is $20, which must be presented with a voucher from CPS, the exam-grading agency.

- Proof of completion of the state-approved course covering Notary laws (for commissions commencing on or after July 1, 2005).

- A completed application form.

- A 2-inch by 2-inch color passport-style photograph of yourself.

- Two sharp #2 black lead pencils.

Items such as backpacks, purses and books are not allowed at the testing tables and must be placed in another location of the room once testing begins. Because neither CPS nor the NNA are responsible for lost or stolen property, the NNA recommends that you leave those belongings in your locked car.

You will receive notice of whether you have passed the exam — results will be mailed within 10 days; scores will not be discussed over the phone.

8. Have your fingerprints electronically scanned.

You must have your fingerprints scanned electronically at a "Live Scan" site. Live Scan fingerprinting services are available at NNA seminars. If you do not attend an NNA seminar or are unable to have your fingerprints taken at the time of the seminar, contact Sylvan/Identix at (800) 315-4507, the NNA at (800) US NOTARY or the state Notary Section at (916) 653-3595 for a listing of Live Scan sites approved by the state Department of Justice. The state Department of Justice Web site (www.ag.ca.gov/fingerprints/publications/contact.htm) also lists Live Scan locations. Call the Live Scan site to determine hours of operation and if an appointment is needed. Bring the Live Scan application, which may be downloaded from the Secretary of State's Web site at www.sos.ca.gov, to the site. A print processing fee of $51 must be paid at the site, along with a print rolling fee that varies according to location. Keep a copy of the Live Scan application until you receive your Notary commission.

9. Receive your new Notary commission.

Usually, within eight to twelve weeks of Live Scan fingerprinting, your application will be processed by the state, and your new Notary commission will be mailed to you, along with a list of licensed seal manufacturers and a Certificate of Authorization allowing you to purchase a seal. If you are a renewing Notary, the new commission will usually be sent to you approximately 30 days before your current commission expires, depending upon when you initiated the application process.

10. File your bond and oath of office.

Within 30 calendar days of the starting date indicated on your commission, you must purchase a $15,000 Notary bond from a licensed surety firm. Both the bond and oath of office must be filed with the clerk of the county in which your principal place of business is located. This can be done either in person or by certified mail if the oath is taken and signed before another Notary Public whose oath and bond have been filed in the same county. Filing fees will vary by county. If you do not file within 30 days, your commission becomes invalid. If that occurs, you must complete a new application and mail it to the Secretary of State's Notary Public Section with a $20 fee; however, you do not have to take the exam again since your exam score is valid for one year.

11. Purchase your official Notary seal.

To purchase an official seal, present or mail the Certificate of Authorization to a licensed seal manufacturer, who will make the seal, affix its impression on the certificate and then return the certificate to the state. You may start using this seal on or after your commission starting date, as long as you have filed your oath and bond with the county clerk and have obtained a journal in which to record your notarial acts. ■

Tools
of the Trade

Notaries need several tools to carry out their duties lawfully and efficiently. Those tools are as important to the Notary as a hammer and saw are to the carpenter.

Inking Seal

The inking seal is the Notary's official seal. Its impression reproduces photographically, a legal requirement. All official acts are authenticated with the seal. It must include the Notary's name, the state seal, the words "Notary Public," the name of the county where the Notary's bond is filed, the commission expiration date, the Notary's commission number and the seal manufacturer or vendor identification number.

Seal Embosser

While not required by California law, the seal embosser is used in many states and is often expected on documents sent abroad. Many California Notaries opt to affix an embossment in addition to the legally required inked-seal impression. The seal embosser makes a nonphotographically reproducible indentation on the document. Because photocopies of documents can sometimes easily pass as originals today, the embossment can be used to distinguish an original from a photocopy. Also, embossing all pages in a document together can safeguard against the substitution or addition of pages.

Journal of Notarial Acts

The Notary's journal is required by law. Each entry must include the date, time and type of each official act; the type of document notarized; the signature of each signer; the type of information used to verify the identity of the parties whose signatures are notarized; the fee charged; and for deeds, quitclaim deeds or deeds of trust affecting real property or powers of attorney, the right thumbprint of the signer. The Notary's journal provides a record of notarial transactions that may be used as evidence in a court proceeding.

Jurat Stamp

The jurat stamp impresses on an affidavit the jurat wording "Subscribed and sworn to before me this _____ day of _____, _____ by _____, proved to me ..." The jurat stamp is more convenient (and safer, since critical wording will not be omitted) than typing the wording on each affidavit that requires it.

Venue Stamp

The venue stamp impresses on the document the phrase, "State of _____, County of _____," which indicates where the notarization took place. The venue stamp may be used when otherwise acceptable notarial wording does not contain a venue statement.

Fingerprinting Device

Since the signers of deeds, quitclaim deeds or deeds of trust affecting real property and all power of attorney documents must leave a right thumbprint in a California Notary's journal, many Notaries opt for the convenience of an inexpensive fingerprinting device.

Notarial Certificates

Preprinted notarial certificates for acknowledgments, jurats, proofs of execution by subscribing witness and copy certification by document custodian are available.

Errors and Omissions Insurance

Notary errors and omissions insurance provides protection for Notaries who are sued for damages resulting from unintentional notarial mistakes. In the event of a lawsuit, the "E&O" insurance company will provide and pay for the Notary's legal counsel and absorb any damages levied by a court or agreed to in a settlement, up to the policy coverage limit. Errors and omissions insurance does not cover the Notary for intentional misconduct. ■

As a full-service organization, the National Notary Association makes available to California Notaries all notarial items required by law, custom and convenience.

10 Most-Asked Questions

Every Notary has a question or two about whether and how to notarize. But certain questions pop up again and again. The following top 10 questions are asked repeatedly at the National Notary Association's seminars, its annual National Conference of Notaries Public and through its Notary Information Service.

As with most questions about notarization, the answer is not always a simple "yes" or "no." Rather, the answer sometimes is, "It depends."

Here is what every Notary wants to know:

1. Can I notarize a will?

It depends. A Notary should only notarize a will if clear instructions and a notarial certificate are provided. If the signer of the will is relying upon the Notary for advice on how to proceed, the Notary should refer the individual to an attorney.

Laws regarding wills differ from state to state. Some states do not require wills to be notarized, while others allow it as one of several witnessing options. Usually, the will itself is not notarized, but accompanying affidavits signed by witnesses typically are.

The danger in notarizing wills is that would-be testators who have drafted their own wills without legal advice may believe that notarization will make their wills legal and valid. However, even when notarized, such homemade wills may be worthless because the testators failed to obtain the proper number of witnesses, or they omitted important information.

In fact, notarization itself may actually void an otherwise properly executed handwritten (holographic) will, because courts have occasionally held that any writing on the document other than the testator's invalidates the will.

2. Can I notarize for a stranger with no identification?

Yes. If identification of a signer cannot be based upon identification documents (ID cards), a Notary may rely upon the oath or affirmation of one personally known credible identifying witness, or two credible identifying witnesses who are strangers to the Notary. Effective January 1, 2008, every credible witness must present a valid state-approved ID to the Notary.

While one personally known credible identifying witness or two unknown witnesses may identify a document signer for an acknowledgment or jurat, a subscribing witness in a proof of execution may only be identified upon the oath or affirmation of one credible witness who is personally known by the Notary and presents the Notary with an acceptable ID.

When a credible identifying witness is not available to identify a stranger without IDs, the Notary might have no choice but to decline the request to notarize.

3. Can I notarize a photograph?

No. To simply stamp and sign a photograph is improper. A Notary's signature and seal must appear only on a notarial certificate (such as an acknowledgment or jurat) accompanying a written statement signed by another person.

However, a signature on a written statement referring to an accompanying or attached photograph may be notarized; if the photograph is large enough, the statement and notarial certificate may even appear on its reverse side. Such formats may be acceptable when notarized photos are requested by persons seeking medical or health licenses, or by legal residents renewing foreign passports.

A word of caution here: A Notary should always be suspicious about notarizing a photo-bearing card or document that could be used as a bogus "official" ID.

4. What if there is no room for my seal or if it smears?

Usually, if notarial wording printed on a document leaves no room for a seal, a loose certificate can be attached and filled out instead.

If an initial seal impression is unreadable and there is ample room on the document, another impression can be affixed nearby. The illegibility of the first impression will indicate why a second seal impression was necessary. The Notary should then record in the journal that a second seal was applied.

A Notary should never attempt to fix an imperfect seal impression with pen, ink or correction fluid. That may be viewed as evidence of tampering and cause the document to be rejected by a receiving agency.

5. Can I notarize signatures on faxes or photocopies of documents?

Yes. A photocopy may be notarized as long as it bears an original signature, meaning that the photocopy must have been signed by hand. A photocopied signature may never be notarized.

Similarly, a faxed document must be signed in ink. In addition, if a faxed document is on thermal paper (the glossy paper used in older fax machines), the document should be photocopied onto regular copy paper to avoid the fading of any printed matter and to allow the affixation of signatures and the Notary's seal.

Note that some public recorders might not accept notarized signatures on photocopied documents because they will not adequately reproduce in microfilming.

6. May I notarize for customers only?

No. As a public official, a Notary is not commissioned to serve just the customers or clients of any one business, even when the employer has paid for the bond, commissioning fees and notarial supplies. There is no such officer as a "Notary Private."

It is ethically improper — although hardly ever explicitly prohibited by statute — to discriminate between customers and noncustomers in offering or refusing to offer notarial services and in charging or not charging fees.

Discrimination against anyone who presents a lawful request for notarization is not a suitable policy for a public official commissioned to serve all of the public equally. Also, such discrimination can provide the basis for lawsuits.

However, California law has a provision whereby a Notary and employer may agree to limit the Notary's services to transactions directly related to the employer's business during business hours. This does not permit discrimination between customers and noncustomers, but only between business-related and nonbusiness-related documents.

7. Can I notarize a document in a language I cannot read?

Yes. As long as the notarial certificate and document signature are in a language the Notary can read, California Notaries may notarize documents written in languages they cannot read.

However, there are certain difficulties and dangers in notarizing documents that the Notary cannot read. The main difficulty for the Notary is making an accurate journal description of an unreadable document; the main danger to the public and the Notary is that the document may be blatantly fraudulent.

Under no circumstances should a notarization be performed if the Notary and the principal signer cannot directly communicate in the same language.

8. Can I certify a copy of a birth certificate?

No. California Notaries are authorized to certify copies only of powers of attorney and, if requested by the Secretary of State, entries in their official journals of notarial acts.

Some states do allow Notaries to certify copies, but copies of documents that are either public records or publicly recordable should never be certified by Notaries. Only an officer in a Bureau of Vital Statistics should certify a copy of a birth certificate or other vital public record; a Notary's "certification" of a birth or death record might actually lend credibility to a counterfeit or altered document. Only a county recording official should certify a copy of a deed or other recordable instrument.

While certifying copies of vital records is prohibited, a Notary may notarize an affidavit of a person requesting a certified copy of a birth or death certificate.

9. Does a document need to be signed in my presence?

It depends. Documents requiring acknowledgments normally do not need to be signed in the Notary's presence. However, the signer must appear before the Notary at the time of notarization to acknowledge that he or she freely signed for the purposes stated in the document. An acknowledgment certificate indicates that the signer personally appeared before the Notary, was identified by the Notary and acknowledged to the Notary that the document was freely signed.

On the other hand, documents requiring a jurat must be signed in the Notary's presence, as dictated by the typical jurat wording, "Subscribed (signed) and sworn to before me ..."

A jurat certificate indicates that the signer personally appeared before the Notary, was identified by the Notary, signed in the Notary's presence and was given an oath or affirmation by the Notary.

10. Can I notarize for a family member?

It depends. Although California state law does not expressly prohibit notarizing for family members, Notaries who do so may violate the statutes prohibiting a direct beneficial interest — especially in notarizing for spouses in states such as California, which has community property laws.

In addition to the possibility of a financial interest in notarizing for a relative, there might be an emotional interest that can prevent the Notary from acting impartially. For example, a Notary who is asked to notarize a contract signed by his or her brother might attempt to persuade the sibling to sign or not sign. As a sibling, the individual is entitled to exert influence — but this is entirely improper for a Notary.

Even if a Notary has no direct beneficial interest in the document and does not attempt to influence the signer, notarizing for a relative could subject the document to a legal challenge if other parties to the transaction allege that the Notary could not have acted impartially. ■

Steps to Proper Notarization

The following 14-step checklist will help Notaries to avoid the most common pitfalls associated with notarization. Always following these guidelines will help shield the Notary from liability in the event that a notarization is challenged.

1. Require every signer to personally appear.

The signer must appear in person before the Notary on the date and in the county stated in the notarial certificate. "Personal appearance" means that the signer is in the Notary's physical presence — face to face in the same room. A telephone call is not acceptable as personal appearance.

2. Make a careful identification.

The Notary should identify every document signer through reliable ID cards or credible identifying witnesses under oath.

When using ID cards, the Notary must examine them closely to detect alteration, counterfeiting or evidence that they are issued to an impostor. Do not rely upon a type of card with which you are unfamiliar, unless you check it against a reference such as the *U.S. Identification Manual* or the *I.D. Checking Guide.*

3. Verify that the signer understands the document.

A conscientious and careful Notary not only will be certain of the signer's identity and willingness to sign, but also will make a layperson's judgment about the signer's ability to understand the document. While California Notaries are not expressly required by law to determine "competence," it is in the Notary's best interest to make a commonsense judgment about the signer's awareness.

A document signer who cannot respond intelligibly in a simple conversation with the Notary should not be considered able to sign at that moment. If in doubt, the Notary may ask the signer if he or she understands the document and can explain its purpose. Or, if in a medical environment, the signer's doctor can be consulted.

4. Check the signature.

The Notary must make sure that the document signer signs the same name appearing on the identification presented.

To check for possible forgery, the Notary should compare the signature that the person leaves in the journal of notarial acts with the signatures on the document and on the IDs. Also, it should be noted whether the signer appears to be laboring on the journal signature, a possible indication of forgery in progress.

Generally, an abbreviated form of a name (John D. Smith instead of John David Smith, for example) is acceptable. However, deviation is only allowed if the individual is signing with less than and not more than what is on the identification document.

5. Look for blank spaces.

California Notaries are expressly prohibited by law from notarizing incomplete documents.

Documents with blank spaces have a great potential for fraudulent misuse. A borrower, for example, might sign an incomplete promissory note, trusting the lender to fill it out, only to discover later that the lender has written in an amount in excess of what was actually borrowed.

If the blanks are inapplicable and intended to be left unfilled, the signer should be asked to line through each space (using ink), or to write in "Not Applicable" or "N/A."

6. Scan the document.

Notaries are not required to read the documents they notarize. However, they should note certain important particulars about a document, such as its title, for recording in the journal of notarial acts. Notaries may also count and record the number of pages; this can show whether pages are later fraudulently added or removed.

7. Check the document's date.

For acknowledgments, the date of signing on the document should either precede or be the same as the date of the notarization but not follow it. For a jurat, the document signing date and the notarization date must be the same.

A document dated after the date on its notarial certificate risks rejection by a recorder, who may question how the document could have been notarized before it was signed.

8. Keep a journal of notarial acts.

A journal is mandatory for all Notaries in California. If a notarized document is lost or altered, or if certain facts about the transaction are later challenged, the Notary's journal becomes valuable evidence. It can protect the rights of all parties to a transaction and help Notaries defend themselves against false accusations.

The Notary should include all of the pertinent details of the notarization in the journal: the date, time and type of notarization; the date and type of document; the address where the notarization was performed; the signature, printed name and address of the signer (and any witnesses); how the signer was identified; and notarial fees charged, if any. In addition, signers of deeds affecting real property or power of attorney documents must leave a right thumbprint in the Notary's journal. Any other pertinent data, such as the capacity the signer is claiming, may also be entered.

9. Complete the journal entry first.

The Notary should complete the journal entry before filling out the notarial certificate. This prevents a signer from leaving before the important public record of the notarization is made in the journal.

10. Make sure the document has notarial wording.

If a notarial certificate does not come with the document, the Notary must ask the document signer what type of notarization — acknowledgment, jurat or other — is required. The Notary may then write or type the appropriate notarial wording on the document or attach a preprinted, "loose" certificate.

If the signer does not know what type of notarization is required, he or she should contact the document's issuing or receiving agency to determine this. This decision is never the

Notary's to make unless the Notary is also an attorney.

11. Be attentive to details.

When completing the certificate, the Notary needs to make sure that the venue statement is present and that it correctly identifies the place of notarization. If the venue statement is absent, the Notary must add it, either by hand or with a venue stamp. If the venue is preprinted and incorrect, the Notary either must line through the incorrect state and/or county and then write in the proper information or must cross out the entire venue statement and then replace it using a venue stamp. In either case, the Notary must initial and date the change.

Also, the Notary must pay attention to spaces on the notarial certificate that indicate the number and gender of the document signers, as well as how they were identified — for example, leave the plural "(s)" untouched or cross it out, as appropriate.

12. Affix your signature and seal properly.

Notaries should sign exactly the same name appearing on their commissioning papers. And they must never forget to affix their official seals — a common reason for rejection of a document by a recorder.

The seal should be placed as close to the Notary's signature as possible without overprinting it. To prevent illegibility, a notarial seal should not be affixed over wording, particularly over a signature.

13. Protect loose certificates.

If the Notary has to attach a notarial certificate, it should be securely attached to the document, usually by stapling the certificate to the left margin of the document's signature page. Notaries can protect against the removal of such attachments by embossing them together with the document and writing the particulars of the document to which the certificate is attached onto the certificate. For example, the notation "This certificate is attached to a 15-page partnership agreement between John Smith and Mary Doe, signed December 16, 2009" would deter fraudulent removal and reattachment of a loose certificate.

14. Do not give advice.

Every state prohibits nonattorneys from practicing law. Notaries should never prepare or complete documents for others or give advice on any matter relating to a document unless they are also attorneys or professionals certified or licensed in a relevant area of expertise. The nonattorney Notary never chooses the type of certificate or notarization a document needs, since this decision can have important legal ramifications. The Notary could be held liable for any damages resulting from an incorrectly chosen certificate or notarization. ■

Notary Laws Explained

In layperson's language, this chapter discusses and clarifies key parts of the state laws that regulate Notaries Public. Most of these laws are reprinted in full in "California Laws Pertaining to Notaries Public" beginning on page 91.

This edition explains the recent changes to California law, including new identification requirements for proofs of execution by subscribing witness.

THE NOTARY COMMISSION

Application for Commission

<u>Qualifications</u>. To become a Notary in California, the applicant (Government Code, Sections 8201, 8201.1, 8201.2 8201.5 and 8214.1):

1) Must be a legal California resident, or a federal civil servant on a military base in accordance with Government Code, Section 8203.1.

2) Must be at least 18 years old.

3) Must complete and pass a proctored, written examination prescribed by the Secretary of State.

4) Must have fingerprints electronically scanned for a background check by the state Department of Justice (DOJ). Effective January 1, 2008, an applicant's fingerprint images must additionally be submitted to the Federal Bureau of Investigation (FBI) for a federal summary of criminal information.

5) Must satisfy the Secretary of State that the applicant is a person of honesty and integrity, and must not have been convicted of a felony or of a crime involving moral turpitude.

6) Is expected to be able to read, write and understand the English language.

7) Is expected to have sufficient vision to read printed matter.

8) Must complete a six-hour education course regarding the Notary's functions and duties. Effective July 1, 2009, renewing Notaries who have completed a state-approved six-hour course and whose commissions have not yet expired must complete a refresher course of at least three hours

9) Must submit a 2-inch by 2-inch color passport-style photograph of his or her person.

State-Residency Requirements. To become a Notary in California, the applicant must be a legal resident of the state. State officials maintain that a legal resident is a person who demonstrates the intent to permanently reside in the state by registering to vote or by obtaining a California driver's license.

A Notary is prohibited from using a commercial mail receiving agency or post office box as a principal place of business or residence unless the applicant also provides a physical street address (Government Code, Section 8213.5).

Citizenship. U.S. citizenship is not required to become a California Notary, though any noncitizen applicant must be a legal resident. A 1984 U.S. Supreme Court decision, *Bernal v. Fainter*, declared that no state may deny a Notary commission merely based on the lack of U.S. citizenship.

Application Fee. The application fee is $40, payable at the site of the proctored exam. Applicants must also pay a $51 print processing fee plus a print-rolling fee at a "Live Scan" fingerprint scanning site. The print-rolling fees vary from location to location. (A listing of Live Scan locations is available online at www.ag.ca.gov/fingerprints/publications/contact.htm.)

Application Misstatement. Substantial and material misstatement or omission in the application for a Notary commission is reason for the Secretary of State to revoke, suspend or refuse to grant a Notary commission (Government Code, Section 8214.1).

Delinquency on Child Support Payments. The Secretary of State is prohibited from issuing or renewing a Notary commission for any person who has not complied with child support orders. Any commission fees that have been paid by the applicant will not be refunded (Welfare and Institutions Code, Section 11350.6).

Dishonored Check. The Secretary of State may cancel the commission of a Notary Public if the commission fee is not paid due to a returned check. Upon receiving notice from a financial institution that a check or draft was not honored, the Secretary of State will notify the applicant and request payment by cashier's check. Should the Secretary of State need to issue a second notice, the commission will be cancelled effective the date of that second notice (Government Code, Section 8204.1).

Examination

Required. All Notary commission applicants — including renewing Notaries — must complete and pass a proctored, written examination prescribed by the Secretary of State.

Cooperative Personnel Services (CPS), a private organization contracted by the state, administers the proctored exam at sites throughout California. For information about taking the exam, contact CPS at (916) 263-3520. For information about taking the exam following an NNA seminar, call (800) 876-6827.

State-Approved Education Course

Required. California law requires Notaries Public appointed on or after July 1, 2005, whether renewing or first time, to have completed an approved six-hour course covering a Notary's duties. Effective July 1, 2009, renewing Notaries who have completed a state-approved six-hour course and whose commissions have not yet expired must complete a refresher course of at least three hours

Fingerprints

Applicants' Prints Electronically Scanned. All Notary commission applicants must have their fingerprints electronically scanned at a Live Scan site. Effective January 1, 2008, renewing

Notaries must also have their fingerprints scanned for each commission renewal (Government Code, Section 8201.1).

Live Scan Sites. Live Scan sites are located throughout the state. To receive a list of designated sites, an applicant may contact the National Notary Association at (800) US NOTARY, the Notary Section at (916) 653-3595 or Sylvan/Identix at (800) 315-4507 or obtain the list online at www.ag.ca.gov/fingerprints/publications/contact.htm.

Applicants should call the Live Scan site in advance to determine the hours of operation and if an appointment is needed. A $51 print processing fee must be paid at the site, along with a print rolling fee that varies according to location.

Notary Bond

Requirement. California Notaries are required to obtain a bond of $15,000 and file it at the office of the county clerk in the county of their principal place of business (Government Code, Section 8212).

Filing the Bond. The bond must be filed along with the oath of office (see "Oath of Office," page 23) within 30 calendar days from the beginning of the Notary's commission term. Notaries may file their bonds in person or by certified mail. The Notary commission does not take effect until the oath and bond are filed. The filing fee varies by county.

The county clerk forwards a copy of the Notary's oath and a certificate, which indicates that the bond was filed, to the Secretary of State. The county clerk then delivers the bond to the county recorder for recording, after which the county recorder mails a copy of the bond to the Notary. The Notary should keep the bond in a safe place for at least six years — the statutory limitation for lawsuits resulting from a notarial act — after the last notarial act performed (Government Code, Section 8213).

Surety. The surety for the Notary's bond must be an approved, state-licensed bonding company. A deposit of funds may not be made in lieu of a surety bond (Government Code, Section 8212).

Protects Public. The Notary bond protects the public, not the Notary, from a Notary's misconduct or negligence. The bond provides coverage for damages to anyone who suffers financially from a Notary's actions — intentional or not. The surety company will seek compensation from the Notary for any damages it has to pay out on the Notary's behalf. The Secretary of State is authorized to require the Notary to purchase replacement bonding if the original $15,000 bond funds are depleted by damage claims.

Liable for All Damages. The Notary and surety company may be sued for damages resulting from notarial misconduct. The surety is liable only up to the amount of the bond, but the Notary may be found liable for any amount of money (Government Code, Section 8214).

Surety's Release from Obligation. If a surety believes that a Notary is likely to perform improper notarial acts in the future, the surety can appeal to the Superior Court for release from the obligation to bond the Notary. A judge may then require proof of the Notary's ability to obtain another surety. If the Notary neglects or refuses to provide a new surety, his or her commission may be revoked (Government Code, Section 8216).

Oath of Office

Requirement. California Notaries are required to take an oath of office and file it with the county clerk in the same county as their principal place of business (Government Code, Sections 8212 and 8213).

Filing the Oath. The oath must be taken and filed along with the Notary bond (see "Notary Bond," pages 22-23) within 30 days from the beginning of the Notary's term. The Notary commission does not take effect until this is done. Notaries may take and file the oath in person at the county clerk's office. Or the oath may be taken before another Notary Public in the same county where it will be filed and mailed by certified mail, along with the proper filing fee, to the county clerk. Filing fees vary by county (Government Code, Section 8213). (For a listing of county clerks, see pages 132–134.)

Jurisdiction

Statewide. Notaries may perform official acts throughout the state of California but not beyond the state borders. A Notary may not witness a signing outside California and then return to the state to perform the notarization. All parts of a notarial act must be performed at the same time and place within the state (Government Code, Section 8200).

Term of Office

Four-Year Term. A Notary's term of office is four years, beginning with the date specified on the commission certificate and ending at midnight on the expiration date (Government Code, Section 8204).

Reappointment

Application for Renewal. To avoid a gap between commissions, Notaries seeking reappointment should begin the application process up to a year before the end of commission. Renewal applications will not be accepted earlier than one year before expiration. Applications are available from the National Notary Association by calling (800) 876-6827 or from Cooperative Personnel Services by calling (916) 263-3520.

Fingerprints. Effective January 1, 2008, a Notary applying for reappointment must submit new prints at a Live Scan electronic scanning site (Government Code, Section 8201.1). (See "Fingerprints," pages 21-22.)

Commission Fees. The fee for a Notary applying for reappointment is $40, just as it is for a first-time applicant.

State-Approved Education. Notaries Public appointed on or after July 1, 2005, whether renewing or first time, must complete a six-hour course covering a Notary's duties. Effective July 1, 2009, renewing Notaries who have completed a state-approved six-hour course and whose commissions have not yet expired must complete a refresher course of at least three hours (Government Code, Section 8201).

Exam Required. All new and renewing Notaries must complete and pass a written examination prescribed by the Secretary of State. (See "Examination," page 21.)

Journal. All California Notaries must maintain a journal of

notarial acts for as long as they hold a Notary Public commission (Government Code, Section 8206).

Renewing Notaries may continue recording their acts in the journal from their previous commission but should make a notation in the journal when the renewed commission begins.

Oath. The oath of office must be taken — and the Notary bond filed — within 30 days from the beginning of the Notary's new commission. The new commission does not take effect until this is done (Government Code, Section 8213).

Bond. All renewing Notaries must obtain a new $15,000 bond (Government Code, Section 8212). (See "Notary Bond," pages 22–23.)

Seal. Renewing Notaries must destroy or deface the seal from their previous commission and obtain a new seal for the new commission. The procedures are the same as if obtaining a seal for the first time. (See "Notary Seal," pages 54–58.)

Resignation

Procedure. To resign, a Notary should immediately notify the Secretary of State by certified mail, destroy or deface the Notary seal and deliver the journal within 30 days to the county clerk of the county where the Notary's bond and oath of office are filed (Government Code, Section 8209). (See "Disposal of Notary Records," page 51.)

Death of Notary

In the case of a Notary's death, his or her personal representative must notify the Secretary of State and deliver all notarial records to the county clerk of the county where the Notary's bond and oath of office are filed (Government Code, Section 8209). The Notary's representative also must destroy or deface the Notary seal (Government Code, Section 8207).

Public-Employee Notaries

Terms of Appointment. The Secretary of State may appoint and issue a Notary commission to state, county, city and public school district employees to act for the agencies in which they are employed. The employing agency may pay the premium on the Notary's bond and the cost of other required supplies from public funds at its disposal (Government Code, Section 8202.5).

No Commission Fees. When a public employee applies for a Notary commission, a signed statement is required from an authorized representative of the agency in which the Notary's services are needed. Provided this statement is filed, no state or county appointment or filing fees need be paid (Government Code, Section 8202.5).

Notary Fees. Any fees collected by a public-employee Notary must be turned over to the agency for which the Notary works. The agency is required to deposit these fees into the same fund from which the Notary's salary is paid (Government Code, Section 8202.5).

Change of Address

Notification. The Secretary of State must be notified by certified mail within 30 days of a change in a Notary's principal place of business or residence address (Government Code, Section 8213.5).

A Notary who willfully fails to notify the Secretary of State of a change of business or residence address is guilty of an infraction and liable for a fine of up to $500 (Government Code, Section 8213.5).

Refile Oath and Bond. Since a Notary has statewide jurisdiction and may notarize in any county, the Notary is not required to refile the oath of office and bond, even if his or her principal place of business moves to a new county. However, the Notary may elect to refile the oath of office and bond in the county of the new principal place of business. If so, then the Notary must also obtain a new official seal that reflects the change within 30 days (Government Code, Section 8213).

Change of Name

Notification Required. A Notary who changes his or her name during the term of the Notary commission must notify the Secretary of State so that the commission may be amended.

A Notary who willfully fails to notify the Secretary of State of a change of name is guilty of an infraction and liable for a fine of up to $500 (Government Code, Section 8213.6).

To amend the commission, the Notary must submit to the Secretary a change of name form, which may be downloaded from the Secretary's Web site at www.sos.ca.gov.

The Secretary of State will issue an amended commission with the Notary's new name. The amended commission takes effect on the date the oath and amendment to the bond are filed with the county clerk (see "File New Oath and Bond Amendment," below). The Notary's commission term and commission number remain the same. The Notary may continue notarizing in the old name until the amended commission takes effect (Government Code, Sections 8213 and 8213.6).

File New Oath and Bond Amendment. After a change of name application is filed, the Notary must also file, within 30 days of the date the amended commission is issued, a new oath of office and an amendment to the bond. The new oath and amended bond are filed with the county clerk of the county in which the Notary's principal place of business is located. The amended commission will not take effect unless the filing is done within the 30-day period (Government Code, Section 8213).

If the address of the Notary's principal place of business was also changed in the "Application for Name Change" form, a new bond (or duplicate of the original) must be filed with the county clerk with an amendment to the bond (Government Code, Section 8213).

New Seal. Within 30 days of filing the new oath and amended bond, the Notary must obtain a new official seal that reflects the name change — and county change, if applicable (Government Code, Section 8213).

OFFICIAL NOTARIAL ACTS

Authorized Acts

Notaries may perform the following notarizations (Government Code, Section 8205):

- Acknowledgments, certifying that a signer personally appeared before the Notary, was identified by the Notary and acknowledged signing the document. (See pages 29–32.)

- <u>Certified Copy of Notarial Record</u>, certifying, when requested by the Secretary of State, that a copy of a requested journal entry is a true copy of that entry. (See pages 32–33.)

- <u>Certified Copy of Power of Attorney</u>, certifying that a copy of a power of attorney document is identical to the original (Probate Code, Section 4307). (See pages 33–34.)

- <u>Depositions</u>, certifying that the spoken words of a witness in a legal matter were accurately taken down in writing, though this act is most often done by skilled court reporters. (See pages 35–36.)

- <u>Jurats</u>, as found in affidavits and other sworn documents, certifying that the signer personally appeared before the Notary, was identified by the Notary, signed in the Notary's presence and took an oath or affirmation from the Notary. (See pages 36–38.)

- <u>Oaths and Affirmations</u>, solemn promises to God (oath) or on one's own personal honor (affirmation). (See pages 38–40.)

- <u>Proofs of Execution</u>, certifying that a subscribing witness personally appeared and swore to the Notary that another person, the principal, signed a document. (See pages 40–42.)

- <u>Protests</u>, certifying that a written promise to pay, such as a bill of exchange, was not honored. (See pages 42–43.)

Unauthorized Acts

<u>Notary's Own Signature</u>. A Notary is not permitted to notarize his or her own signature (Government Code, Section 8224.1).

<u>Certified Copies</u>. A certified copy is a duplicate of an original document that is certified as an exact reproduction. In California, a Notary is prohibited from making certified copies of anything but the Notary's own official journal or a power of attorney document (Government Code, Section 8205). (See "Certified Copies of Notarial Records," pages 32-33, and "Certified Copies of Powers of Attorney," pages 33–34.)

Requests for certified copies of any other document should be directed to the agency that holds the original document. For certified copies of birth, death or marriage certificates and other vital records, the person requesting the certified copy should be referred to the appropriate Bureau of Vital Statistics. (See "Bureaus of Vital Statistics," pages 135–139.)

Acknowledgments

Purpose. Acknowledgments are one of the most common forms of notarization. Typically, they are executed on deeds and other documents affecting real property that will be publicly recorded by a county recorder.

In executing an acknowledgment, a Notary certifies three things (Civil Code, Section 1185):

1) The signer personally appeared before the Notary on the date and in the state and county indicated on the notarial certificate. (Notarization cannot be based upon a telephone call or on a Notary's familiarity with a signature.)

2) The signer was positively identified by the Notary through satisfactory evidence. (See "Identifying Document Signers," pages 43–47.)

3) The signer acknowledged to the Notary that the signature was freely made for the purposes stated in the document. (If a document is willingly signed in the presence of the Notary, this act can serve just as well as an oral statement of acknowledgment.)

Certificate for Acknowledgment. For every acknowledgment on a document that will be filed in California, regardless of whom the signer is representing, a California Notary must use the exact wording in the following "all-purpose" certificate (Civil Code, Sections 1188 and 1189):

State of California   )
)
County of _____   )

On _____ before me, (here insert name and title of the officer), personally appeared _____
_____, who proved to me on the basis of satisfactory evidence to be the person(s) whose name(s) is/are subscribed to the within instrument and acknowledged to me that he/she/they executed the same in his/her/their authorized capacity(ies), and that

by his/her/their signature(s) on the instrument the person(s), or the entity upon behalf of which the person(s) acted, executed the instrument.

I certify under PENALTY OF PERJURY under the laws of the State of California that the foregoing paragraph is true and correct.

WITNESS my hand and official seal.

Signature _____ (Seal)

Any lawful acknowledgment form executed before January 1, 1993, will be honored (Civil Code, Section 1189).

Penalty of Perjury. Effective January 1, 2008, Notaries must sign all California "all-purpose" acknowledgment certificates under penalty of perjury (Civil Code, Section 1189).

Certificate for Documents Filed Out of State. A California Notary may complete an acknowledgment certificate prescribed by or used in a U.S. state or jurisdiction other than California only if the document will be filed outside of California.

However, an out-of-state certificate may not be used if it requires the Notary to make any determination or certification not allowed by California law, such as certifying a signer's particular representative capacity as attorney in fact, corporate officer or other status. The out-of-state certificate may refer to the capacity claimed by the signer, but the Notary may not certify that the signer does, in fact, have the authority to sign under the claimed capacity (Civil Code, Section 1189).

Identification of Acknowledger. In an acknowledgment, the Notary must identify the signer through satisfactory evidence consisting of either a credible identifying witness(es) or identification documents (Civil Code, Section 1185). (See "Identifying Document Signers," pages 43–47.)

Witnessing Signature Not Required. For an acknowledgment, the document does not have to be signed in the Notary's presence. However, the signer must appear before the Notary at the time of notarization to acknowledge having signed the document.

A document may have been signed an hour before, a week before, a year before, etc. — as long as the signer appears before the Notary with the signed document at the time of notarization to acknowledge that the signature is his or her own. (Conversely, for a jurat requiring an oath or affirmation, the document must be signed in the Notary's presence. See "Jurats," pages 36–38.)

Failure to Complete Acknowledgment. Failure to complete an acknowledgment at the same time that the Notary's signature and seal are affixed to the document is reason for the Secretary of State to revoke, suspend or refuse to grant a Notary's commission. In addition, a fine of up to $750 may be imposed (Government Code, Sections 8214.1 and 8214.15).

False Certificate. A Notary is liable for a civil penalty of up to $10,000 for willfully stating as true any material fact in an acknowledgment certificate that he or she knows is false. This penalty may be imposed either by the Secretary of State in an administrative hearing or by a public prosecutor in superior court (Civil Code, Section 1185[b][1][B]).

Out-of-State Acknowledgment. Acknowledgment certificates completed outside of California by Notaries of another state in accordance with the laws of that state may be recorded in California (Civil Code, Section 1189).

Terminology. In discussing acknowledgments, it is important to use proper terms. A Notary takes or executes an acknowledgment, while a document signer makes or gives an acknowledgment.

Who May Take. Within the state, Notaries and the following officials may take acknowledgments and proofs of execution in their jurisdictions (Civil Code, Section 1181):

- Clerks of superior, municipal and justice courts and clerks of boards of supervisors, counties and cities

- Court commissioners; municipal, justice court and retired judges; county counsels.

- District and city attorneys

Outside of California, but within the United States and its jurisdictions, acknowledgments and proofs of execution may be made before any of the following (Civil Code, Section 1182):

- A Notary Public

- A judge, justice or clerk of any court of record of the United States

- A commissioner appointed by the Governor or Secretary of State

- Any other authorized officer

Outside of the United States, acknowledgments and proofs may be made before the following officials (Civil Code, Section 1183):

- A Notary Public, providing that the Notary's signature is proven before a judge of a court of record where the notarization is performed, by any American diplomatic officer or authorized consular agent or by *apostille*

- A judge of a court of record, a consul, vice consul or consular agent of the U.S. in the foreign jurisdiction

- A commissioner appointed by the Governor or by the Secretary of State

Certified Copies of Notarial Records

<u>Secretary of State Request</u>. Upon receipt of a written request from the Secretary of State, a Notary must furnish a certified copy of the requested journal entry within the time specified in the request (Government Code, Section 8205[b][1]).

Notary must provide his or her notarial journal
d photocopying upon receipt of a subpoena
urt order. The copying must be performed in
Notary, and the Notary must certify the copies
nment Code, Section 8206).

Public and Employer Request. A Notary must provide a journal entry photocopy — not a certified copy — to any member of the public or an employer under certain circumstances. (See "Journal-Entry Copies" and "Copying by Employer," pages 49-50.)

Certificate for Certified Copy of Notarial Record. California law does not provide certificate wording for Notaries issuing certified copies of journal entries. The National Notary Association recommends the following form:

State of California   )
) ss.
County of _____)

On this the _____ day of _____ (month), _____ (year), I,
_____ (name of Notary Public), the undersigned Notary Public,
hereby declare that the attached reproduction of a Notary journal entry
involving _____ (describe document, noting date and
signer[s]) is a true and correct photocopy made from a page in my Notary
journal.

_____ (Signature of Notary)   (Seal of Notary)

Certified Copies of Powers of Attorney

Procedure. In addition to notarizing signatures on powers of attorney, Notaries may certify copies of such documents. The Notary compares the copy to the original to verify that the copy is, in fact, identical to the original power of attorney document. Ideally, the Notary should personally make the photocopy that is to be certified to ensure that the copy is identical to the original (Government Code, Section 8205 and Probate Code, Section 4307).

Certificate for Certified Copy of Power of Attorney. A certificate for a certified copy of a power of attorney must state that the Notary has examined the original power of attorney and the copy and has determined that the copy is a true and correct copy of the original power of attorney (Probate Code, Section 4307[c]). The National Notary Association recommends the following wording for Notaries certifying copies of powers of attorney:

State of California   )
) ss.
County of _____   )

On this the _____ day of _____ (month), _____
(year), I, _____ (name of Notary Public), the undersigned Notary
Public, hereby certify that the attached document is a true, complete and
unaltered photocopy of a power of attorney presented to me on this date
by _____ (presenter's name), under Section 4307 of the California
Probate Code.

_____ (Signature of Notary)   (Seal of Notary)

Journal Entry. The Notary must complete a journal entry for a copy certification of a power of attorney document.

Identification of Presenter. Although not required by law, the Notary should properly identify the document presenter by the same identification standards prescribed for acknowledgments.

Copy Certification by Document Custodian

Purpose. Because California Notaries are not allowed to certify copies of any document except powers of attorney and journal records, copy certification by document custodian may often serve as an acceptable alternative when a Notary-certified copy (permitted in many other states and countries) is requested. Copy certification by document custodian may not be acceptable to the individual or agency receiving the copy, so the person requesting the act should verify that it will serve the required purposes.

Procedure. The permanent keeper of the document — the document custodian — certifies the copy, not the Notary. The custodian makes a photocopy of the original document, makes a written statement about the trueness, correctness and completeness of the copy, signs that statement before a Notary, is identified by the Notary and takes an oath or affirmation regarding the truthfulness of the statement. The Notary, having witnessed the signing, identified the signer through satisfactory evidence and administered the oath or affirmation, executes a jurat.

Not for Vital Records. Copy certification by document custodian is not appropriate for vital records such as birth, marriage and death certificates, since originals of these documents are retained by public agencies. Persons requesting certified copies of vital records should be directed to the agency that holds the original — typically, the Bureau of Vital Statistics or county clerk where the birth, death or marriage occurred.

However, effective July 1, 2003, Notaries may notarize an affidavit of a person requesting a certified copy of a birth or death certificate. They still cannot certify such records, however (California Health and Safety Code, Section 103526).

Certificate for Copy Certification by Document Custodian. In addition to the jurat certificate, the custodian's statement is required. Although not prescribed by law, the following wording — which includes the required jurat — is recommended by the National Notary Association:

I, _____ (name of custodian of original document), hereby swear (or affirm) that the attached reproduction of _____ (description of original document) is a true, correct and complete photocopy of a document in my possession.

_____ (signature of custodian)
_____ (address)

State of California   )
)
County of _____)

Subscribed and sworn to (or affirmed) before me on this _____ day of _____ (month), _____ (year), by _____, proved to me on the basis of satisfactory evidence to be the person(s) who appeared before me.

_____ (Signature of Notary)   (Seal of Notary)

Depositions and Affidavits

Purpose. A deposition is a signed transcript of the signer's oral statements taken down for use in a judicial proceeding. The deposition signer is called the deponent.

An affidavit is a signed statement made under oath or affirmation by a person called an affiant, and it is used for a variety of purposes both in and out of court.

For either one, the Notary must administer an oath or affirmation and complete a jurat, which the Notary signs and seals.

Depositions. With a deposition, both sides in a lawsuit or court case have the opportunity to cross-examine the deponent. Questions and answers are transcribed into a written statement. Used only in judicial proceedings, a deposition is then signed and sworn to or affirmed before an oath-administering official.

California Notaries have the power to take depositions — meaning, to transcribe the words spoken aloud by a deponent — but this duty is most often executed by trained and certified court reporters.

Affidavits. Affidavits are used in and out of court for a variety of purposes, from declaring losses to an insurance company to declaring U.S. citizenship before traveling to a foreign country. An affidavit is a document containing a statement voluntarily signed and sworn to or affirmed before a Notary or other official with oath-administering powers. If used in a judicial proceeding, only one side in the case need participate in the execution of the affidavit, unlike with the deposition.

Certificate for Depositions and Affidavits. Depositions and affidavits require jurat certificates. (See "Jurats," pages 36–38.)

Oath (Affirmation) for Depositions and Affidavits. If no other wording is prescribed in a given instance, a Notary may use the following language in administering an oath (or affirmation) for an affidavit or deposition:

> Do you solemnly swear that the statements made in this affidavit (or deposition) are the truth, the whole truth and nothing but the truth, so help you God?

> (Do you solemnly affirm that the statements made in this affidavit [or deposition] are the truth, the whole truth and nothing but the truth?)

Response Required. For an oath or affirmation, the affiant must respond aloud and affirmatively, with "I do," "Yes" or the like.

e. In notarizing affidavits, depositions and other forms
erification requiring an oath or affirmation by the
tary normally executes a jurat.

The purpose of a jurat is to compel truthfulness by appealing to the signer's conscience and fear of criminal penalties for perjury. In executing a jurat, a Notary certifies four things:

1) The signer personally appeared before the Notary at the time of notarization on the date and in the state and county indicated. (Notarization based upon a telephone call or on familiarity with a signature is not acceptable.)

2) The signer was positively identified by the Notary through satisfactory evidence (see "Identifying Document Signers," pages 43–47).

3) The Notary watched the signature being made at the time of notarization.

4) The Notary administered an oath or affirmation to the signer.

Identification. In a jurat, the Notary must identify the signer based on satisfactory evidence (Government Code, Section 8202[a]). (See "Identifying Document Signers," pages 43–47.)

Certificate for a Jurat. California Notaries may only use jurat wording exactly as prescribed in statute. If the venue is separated from otherwise acceptable jurat wording, the Notary should line through the venue, initial and date the correction and write or stamp the new venue above the certificate. California law prescribes a certificate for a jurat (Government Code, Section 8202[b]):

State of California   )
)
County of _____)

Subscribed and sworn to (or affirmed) before me on this _____ day of _____ (month), _____ (year), by _____, proved to me on the basis of satisfactory evidence to be the person(s) who appeared before me.

_____ (Signature of Notary)   (Seal of Notary)

Verifying Age. In executing a jurat on a document that includes the signer's date of birth or age and the signer's photograph or fingerprint, the Notary must verify the date of birth or age through a birth certificate, a state driver's license or a nondriver's ID (Government Code, Section 8230).

Wording for Jurat Oath (Affirmation). If not otherwise prescribed by law, a California Notary may use the following or similar words to administer an oath (or affirmation) in conjunction with a jurat:

> Do you solemnly swear that the statements in this document are true to the best of your knowledge and belief, so help you God?

> (Do you solemnly affirm that the statements in this document are true to the best of your knowledge and belief?)

Oath or Affirmation Not Administered. Failure to administer any oath or affirmation as required by law is reason for the Secretary of State to revoke, suspend or refuse to grant a Notary commission. In addition, a fine of up to $750 may be imposed (Government Code, Sections 8214.1 and 8214.15).

Oaths and Affirmations

Purpose. An oath is a solemn, spoken pledge to a Supreme Being. An affirmation is a solemn, spoken pledge on one's own personal honor, with no reference to a Supreme Being. Both are usually a promise of truthfulness and have the same legal effect.

In taking an oath or affirmation in an official proceeding, a person may be subject to criminal penalties for perjury should he or she fail to be truthful.

An oath or affirmation can be a full-fledged notarial act in its own right, as when giving an oath of office to a public official (when "swearing in" a public official), or it can be part of the process of notarizing a document (e.g., executing a jurat or swearing in a subscribing witness).

A person who objects to taking an oath may instead be given an affirmation.

Power to Administer. California Notaries and certain other officers are authorized to administer oaths and affirmations (Code of Civil Procedure, Section 2093).

Wording for Oath (Affirmation). If state law does not dictate otherwise, a California Notary may use the following or similar words in administering an oath (or affirmation):

- Oath (Affirmation) for an affiant signing an affidavit:

    Do you solemnly swear that the statements in this document are true to the best of your knowledge and belief, so help you God?

    (Do you solemnly affirm that the statements in this document are true to the best of your knowledge and belief?)

- Oath (Affirmation) for a witness testifying in a court case (Code of Civil Procedure, Section 2094):

    Do you solemnly swear that the evidence you shall give in this issue (or matter), pending between (first party) and (second party), shall be the truth, the whole truth and nothing but the truth, so help you God?

    (Do you solemnly affirm that the evidence you shall give in this issue [or matter], pending between [first party] and [second party], shall be the truth, the whole truth and nothing but the truth?)

- Oath (Affirmation) for a credible identifying witness (Civil Code, Section 1185):

    Do you solemnly swear that (signer) is the person named in the document; that (signer) is personally known to you; that it is your reasonable belief that the circumstances of (signer) are such that it would be very difficult or impossible for him/her to obtain another form of identification; that (signer) does not possess any of the acceptable identification documents; and that you do not have a financial interest nor are you named in the document, so help you God?

    (Do you solemnly affirm that [signer] is the person named in the document; that [signer] is personally known to you; that it is your reasonable belief that the circumstances of [signer] are such that it would be very difficult or impossible for him/her to obtain another form of identification; that [signer] does not possess any of the acceptable identification documents; and that you do not have a financial interest nor are you named in the document?)

- Oath (Affirmation) for a subscribing witness:

    Do you solemnly swear that you saw (name of the document signer) sign his/her name to this document and/or that he/she acknowledged to you having executed it for the purposes therein stated, so help you God?

(Do you solemnly affirm that you saw [name of the document signer] sign his/her name to this document and/or that he/she acknowledged to you having executed it for the purposes therein stated?)

Response Required. The oath or affirmation wording must be spoken aloud, and the person taking the oath or affirmation must answer affirmatively with "I do," "Yes" or the like. A nod or grunt is not a clear and sufficient response. If a person is unable to speak, the Notary may rely upon written notes to communicate.

Ceremony and Gestures. To impress upon the oath-taker or affirmant the importance of truthfulness, the Notary is encouraged to lend a sense of ceremony and formality to the oath or affirmation. During the administration of an oath or affirmation, the Notary and document signer may raise their right hands, though this is not a legal requirement. Notaries generally have discretion to use words and gestures they feel will most compellingly appeal to the conscience of the oath-taker or affirmant.

Oath or Affirmation Not Administered. Failure to administer any oath or affirmation as required by law is reason for the Secretary of State to revoke, suspend or refuse to grant a Notary commission. In addition, a fine of up to $750 may be imposed (Government Code, Sections 8214.1 and 8214.15).

Proof of Execution by Subscribing Witness

Purpose. In executing a proof of execution, a Notary certifies that the signature of a person who does not appear before the Notary — the principal signer — is genuine and freely made based upon the sworn testimony of another person who does appear: a subscribing (signing) witness.

Proofs of execution are used when the principal signer does not appear before a Notary. Because of their high potential for fraudulent abuse, proofs should only be used as a last resort and never merely because the principal signer prefers not to take the time to personally appear before a Notary.

In Lieu of Acknowledgment. On recordable documents, a proof of execution is usually regarded as an acceptable substitute for an acknowledgment (Civil Code, Section 1195).

Limitations. Proofs of execution are not permitted with mortgages, deeds of trust, security agreements, quitclaim deeds and grant deeds, but are allowed with trustee's deeds resulting from foreclosure and deeds of reconveyance (Government Code, Section 27287 and Civil Code, Section 1195).

Subscribing Witness. A subscribing witness is a person who watches a principal sign a document (or who personally takes the principal's acknowledgment) and then subscribes (signs) his or her own name on the document. This witness brings that document to a Notary on the principal's behalf and takes an oath or affirmation from the Notary to the effect that the principal did willingly sign (or acknowledge signing) the document.

The ideal subscribing witness personally knows the principal signer and has no beneficial interest in the document or transaction. It would be foolish of the Notary, for example, to rely upon the word of a subscribing witness presenting for notarization a power of attorney that names this very witness as attorney in fact.

Oath (Affirmation) for a Subscribing Witness. An acceptable oath for the subscribing witness might be:

Do you solemnly swear that you saw (name of the document signer) sign his/her name to this document and/or that he/she acknowledged to you having executed it for the purposes therein stated, so help you God?

(Do you solemnly affirm that you saw [name of the document signer] sign his/her name to this document and/or that he/she acknowledged to you having executed it for the purposes therein stated?)

The subscribing witness then signs the Notary's journal and the Notary completes a proof of execution by subscribing witness certificate, often called a witness jurat.

Identifying the Subscribing Witness. The subscribing witness's identity must be proved on the oath of one credible identifying witness who is personally known to the Notary. The credible witness also must present a valid state-approved ID card to the Notary (Civil Code, Section 1196).

Certificate for Proof of Execution. While Civil Code Section 1195 contains a statutory certificate for a proof of execution by subscribing witness, the changes brought about by Chapter 67 of the Laws of 2007 have rendered that certificate inaccurate. Therefore, the Secretary of State recommends that Notaries use the following or similar wording when performing a proof of execution by subscribing witness:

State of California   ) ss.
County of _____)

On _____ (date), before me, the undersigned, a notary public for the state, personally appeared _____ (subscribing witness's name), proved to me to be the person whose name is subscribed to the within instrument, as a witness thereto, on the oath of _____ (credible witness's name), a credible witness who is known to me and provided a satisfactory identifying document. _____ (subscribing witness's name) being by me duly sworn, deposed and said that he/she was present and saw/heard _____ (name(s) of principal(s)), the same person(s) described in and whose name(s) is/are subscribed to the within, or attached, instrument in his/her/their authorized capacity(ies) as (a) party(ies) thereto, execute or acknowledge executing the same, and that said affiant subscribed his/her name to the within instrument as a witness at the request of _____ (name(s) of principal(s)).

WITNESS my hand and official seal.

_____
Notary Public Signature
Notary Public Seal

Do Not Use All-Purpose Acknowledgment Form. The so-called "all-purpose" acknowledgment certificate, prescribed in Civil Code Section 1189, should not be used for proofs of execution by subscribing witness.

Protests

Purpose. In rare instances, Notaries might be asked to protest a negotiable instrument for nonpayment. A protest is a written statement by a Notary or other authorized officer verifying that payment was not received on an instrument such as a bank draft. Failure to pay is called dishonor. Before issuing a certificate of protest, the Notary must present the bank draft or other instrument to the person or entity obliged to pay, a procedure called presentment (Uniform Commercial Code, Section 3505).

Antiquated Act. In the 19th century, protests were

common notarial acts in the United States, but they are rarely performed today due to the advent of modern electronic communications and resulting changes in our banking and financial systems. Modern Notaries most often encounter protests in the context of international commerce.

Special Knowledge Required. Notarial acts of protest are complicated and varied, requiring a special knowledge of financial and legal terminology. Only Notaries who have the requisite special knowledge, or who are acting under the supervision of an experienced bank officer or an attorney familiar with the Uniform Commercial Code, should attempt to execute a protest.

Certificate for Protest. When a Notary protests a promissory note or bill of exchange for nonpayment or nonacceptance, the protest certificate must include the following (Government Code, Section 8208):

1) The time and place of presentment of the bill or note.

2) That presentment was made and how presentment was made.

3) The cause or reason for protesting the bill or note.

4) The demand made and the answer given, if any, or the fact that the drawee or acceptor could not be found.

Protests from Out of State. When protesting bills of exchange or promissory notes, a California Notary may exercise any additional customary powers and duties prescribed by the other state or nation for that protest. This authorization applies only to protests and not any other notarial act (Government Code, Section 8205).

PRACTICES AND PROCEDURES

Identifying Document Signers

Satisfactory Evidence. In taking acknowledgments and executing jurats for any document, California law requires the Notary to identify the acknowledger or affiant. The following two methods of identification constitute satisfactory evidence (Civil Code, Section 1185):

1) Reliable identification documents or ID cards (See "Identification Documents," pages 44–45.)

2) The oath or affirmation of one personally known or two unknown credible identifying witnesses. (See "Credible Identifying Witness(es)," pages 46–47.)

Verifying Representative Capacity. The California Notary is not required or authorized to verify the capacity in which a person signs — such as corporate officer, trustee, partner to a partnership, attorney in fact or other representative capacity. The Notary only identifies the acknowledging signer as an individual (Civil Code, Section 1189[2][c]).

Personal Knowledge of Identity

No Longer Acceptable. Effective January 1, 2008, Notaries may no longer use personal knowledge to identify a signer of an acknowledgment or jurat. Furthermore, effective January 1, 2009, Notaries may no longer use personal knowledge to identify a subscribing witness (Civil Code, Sections 1185 and 1196).

Identification Documents (ID Cards)

Acceptable Identification Documents. A Notary may identify a document signer for an acknowledgment or jurat based on an identification document that meets the following criteria (Civil Code, Section 1185):

- Current or, if expired, issued within the past five years

- Contains the document signer's photograph, physical description and signature

- Bears a serial or other identifying number

California Notaries may only accept the following types of identification documents:

- California driver's license or nondriver's ID issued by the California Department of Motor Vehicles

- U.S. passport book or card (A physical description is not required, and the passport card is acceptable even though it does not contain the bearer's signature.)

- Foreign passport stamped by the U.S. Citizenship and Immigration Services (USCIS)

- Driver's license or nondriver's ID issued by another U.S. state

- Driver's license issued by Mexico or Canada

- Employee ID card issued by an agency or office of the State of California or any city, county or city and county within the state

- U.S. military ID that contains all required elements (The Common Access Card [CAC] — a replacement ID for certain military personnel — does not contain the signature of the bearer on either the front or back of the card. Therefore, under current law, California Notaries may not accept the CAC as identification for notarizations.)

- Inmate ID issued by the California Department of Corrections (Inmate ID cards may only be used to identify prisoners who are in custody.)

- ID cards issued by the USCIS (USCIS IDs may only be used to identify signers for notarizations on USCIS forms.) (Government Code, Section 8230)

Unacceptable Identification Documents. Identification documents that are not acceptable for identifying signers include Social Security cards, credit cards, temporary driver's licenses and driver's licenses without photographs.

Multiple Identification. While one good identification document may be sufficient to identify a signer, the Notary may ask for more.

Credible Identifying Witness(es)

Purpose. When a document signer is unable to present reliable ID cards, that signer may be identified on the oath (or affirmation) of one or two credible identifying witness(es) (Civil Code, Section 1185).

Qualifications. Every credible identifying witness must personally know the document signer.

A credible identifying witness must not have an interest, or be named, in the document. A credible identifying witness must know that the signer has no identification and that it would be impractical to obtain the necessary ID (Civil Code, Section 1185).

Credible Witness(es) Must Present ID. Effective January 1, 2008, every credible witness — known or unknown to the Notary — must present a valid state-approved ID card to the Notary. Previously, only credible witnesses who were unknown to the Notary were required to present ID.

A Notary who fails to require a personally known credible witness to present a valid state-approved ID is liable for a civil penalty of up to $10,000. This penalty may be brought by the Secretary of State in an administrative hearing or by a public prosecutor in superior court (Civil Code, Section 1185[b][1][B]).

Oath (Affirmation) for Credible Identifying Witness. To ensure truthfulness, the Notary must administer an oath or affirmation to each credible identifying witness. The credible identifying witness must swear or affirm that the following are true (Civil Code, Section 1185):

- The person making the acknowledgment or oath (affirmation) is the person named in the document.

- The person making the acknowledgment or oath (affirmation) is personally known to the witness.

- The person making the acknowledgment or oath (affirmation) does not possess any of the acceptable identification documents.

- That the witness believes it is very difficult or impossible for the person making the acknowledgment or oath (affirmation) to obtain another form of identification.

- The witness does not have a financial interest in the document and is not named in the document.

An acceptable oath (affirmation) for a credible identifying witness might be:

> Do you solemnly swear that (signer) is the person named in the document; that (signer) is personally known to you; that it is your reasonable belief that the circumstances of (signer) are such that it would be very difficult or impossible for him/her to obtain another form of identification; that (signer) does not possess any of the acceptable identification documents; and that you do not have a financial interest, nor are you named, in the document, so help you God?

> (Do you solemnly affirm that [signer] is the person named in the document; that [signer] is personally known to you; that it is your reasonable belief that the circumstances of [signer] are such that it would be very difficult or impossible for him/her to obtain another form of identification; that [signer] does not possess any of the acceptable identification documents; and that you do not have a financial interest, nor are you named, in the document?)

Signature and ID in Notary's Journal. Each credible identifying witness must sign the Notary's journal, along with the document signer. The Notary must indicate how the credible identifying witness was identified. Previously, only credible witnesses who were not personally known to the Notary were required to present ID. Now, all credible witnesses must present state-approved ID documents. The Notary Public must record each credible witness's identification information including the type of identification document used, the serial or identifying number and the date of issuance or expiration (Government Code, Section 8206).

While the law does not require a Notary to record the ID card information in the journal for one personally known credible witness, the National Notary Association recommends that the Notary include this information as well.

Not a Subscribing Witness. Do not confuse credible identifying witnesses with subscribing witnesses. A credible identifying witness vouches for the identity of a signer who appears before the Notary. A subscribing witness vouches for the genuineness of the signature of a person who does not appear before the Notary. (See "Proof of Execution by Subscribing Witness," pages 40–42.)

Journal of Notarial Acts

Requirement. California Notaries are required to keep one

active sequential journal of all of their official acts. A permanently bound record book (not loose-leaf) with numbered pages and entry spaces is best for preserving the sequence of notarial acts and for protecting against unauthorized removal of pages or tampering (Government Code, Section 8206).

Security of Journal. The journal must be kept in a locked and secured area under direct supervision and control of the Notary (Government Code, Section 8206).

Failure to secure the journal is reason for the Secretary of State to revoke, suspend or refuse to grant a Notary commission. In addition, a fine of up to $750 may be imposed (Government Code, Sections 8214.1 and 8214.15).

Failure to Keep. Failure to keep a journal of notarial acts is reason for the Secretary of State to revoke, suspend or refuse to grant a Notary commission. In addition, a fine may be imposed. A Notary who willfully fails to properly maintain a journal of official acts is guilty of a misdemeanor (Government Code, Sections 8214.1, 8214.15 and 8228.1).

Journal Entries. For each notarization, the journal must contain the following entries (Government Code, Section 8206):

1) The date, time of day and type of notarization (jurat, acknowledgment, etc.).

2) The type of document notarized (deed of trust, affidavit of support, etc.).

3) The signature of each person whose signature is notarized, including the signature of any subscribing witness.

4) A statement as to how the signer's identity was confirmed. The journal entry must contain either a description of the ID card accepted (including the type of ID, the government agency issuing the ID, the serial or identifying number and the date of issuance or expiration) or the signature(s) of the credible identifying witness(es) and the ID card information for the witness(es). (See "Credible Identifying Witness(es)," pages 45–47.)

5) The fee charged for the notarial service.

6) For deeds, quitclaim deeds and deeds of trust affecting any real property and all powers of attorney, the right thumbprint of each signer. (See "Journal Thumbprint Requirement," below.)

Journal Thumbprint Requirement. All signers of all powers of attorney as well as deeds, quitclaim deeds and deeds of trust affecting any real property must leave a right thumbprint in the Notary's journal of notarial acts. A journal thumbprint is not required of signers of deeds of reconveyance and trustee's deeds resulting from a decree of foreclosure or a nonjudicial foreclosure (Government Code, Section 8206).

If the signer's right thumbprint is not available, the Notary is required to obtain the left thumbprint or a print of any available finger. The Notary must note this in the journal. If the signer is physically unable to leave a thumbprint or a fingerprint, the Notary must note this in the journal with an explanation of the signer's physical condition (Government Code, Section 8206).

The journal thumbprint is a strong deterrent to forgery because it represents absolute proof of the forger's identity. Nothing prevents a Notary from asking for a thumbprint for every notarial act, if the signer is willing. It can only be made a precondition for notarizing when the document is a deed, quitclaim deed or deed of trust affecting real estate or a power of attorney document.

Failure to Obtain Thumbprint. A Notary who willfully fails to obtain a thumbprint in the journal as required by law is subject to a civil penalty of up to $2,500. This fine may be brought either by the Secretary of State in an administrative hearing or by a public prosecutor in superior court (Government Code, Section 8214.23).

Journal-Entry Copies. The law requires a Notary to provide a photocopy of a journal line item entry to any member of the public who presents a written request specifying the names of the parties, the type of document and the month and year the document was notarized (Government Code, Section 8206[c]).

Effective January 1, 2008, Government Code Section 8206.5 stipulates that, within 15 business days of receipt of a written request to provide a photocopy of an entry, a Notary must provide the requested photocopy or acknowledge that no such line item exists.

In a disciplinary proceeding for failure to provide either the line item or a response within 15 business days, a Notary may defend his or her delayed action on the basis of unavoidable, exigent business or personal circumstances (Government Code Section 8206.5).

Copying by Employer. An employer of a Notary may request inspection or copies of journal entries that are directly related to the employer's business if the inspection or copying is done in the Notary's presence. An employer may ask a Notary-employee to regularly provide copies of business-related entries from the journal. The confidentiality and safekeeping of such journal copies are the employer's responsibility. The Notary shall not be required to allow inspection or provide copies of journal entries that are not related to the employer's business (Government Code, Section 8206[d]).

Surrendering Journal. Notaries should never surrender control of their official journals to anyone. Even when an employer has paid for the Notary's official journal — and regardless of whether the journal contains entries related to the employer's business — the journal stays with the Notary upon termination of employment; no person but the Notary can lawfully possess and use this official recordbook (Government Code, Section 8206).

Law Enforcement Access. A peace officer who has reasonable suspicion or probable cause to believe the journal contains evidence of a crime may request the Notary to surrender the journal. A Notary must surrender the journal to the peace officer immediately, or if the journal is not present as soon as possible thereafter (Government Code, Sections 8206[d] and [f]).

A peace officer who has probable cause that the journal contains evidence of a criminal act may seize the journal. Any requirements of, or exceptions to, state and federal law shall apply to an officer who seizes a journal (Government Code, Section 8206[d]).

A peace officer is defined by Penal Code Sections 830.1, 830.2 and 830.3. (See "California Laws Pertaining to Notaries Public," pages 91-130)

A Notary may be fined up to $2,500 for willfully failing to provide access to the journal when requested by a peace officer. This fine may be imposed by the Secretary of State in an administrative proceeding or a public prosecutor in superior court (Government Code, Section 8214.21).

If Notary Journal is Seized. If the Notary's journal is seized by a peace officer, the Notary must obtain a receipt for the relinquished journal from the peace officer and notify the Secretary of State by certified mail within 10 days. The notification must include the period of the journal entries, the Notary's commission number and expiration date, and a photocopy of the receipt. Upon surrendering the journal to a peace officer, the Notary must obtain a new journal, and if the seized journal is returned, the Notary may not use it to record any new entries (Government Code, Section 8206[d]).

Lost or Stolen Journal. A Notary must immediately notify the Secretary of State by certified or registered mail if a journal is lost, stolen, misplaced, destroyed, damaged or otherwise rendered unusable. When notifying, the Notary must include his or her commission number and expiration date, the time period covered by the journal entries and a photocopy of any relevant police report (Government Code, Section 8206).

Destruction of Notary Records. It is a misdemeanor for any person to purposely destroy, deface or conceal a Notary's journal. A person who does so is liable for damages suffered by any person as a result (Government Code, Sections 8209 and 8221).

Disposal of Notary Records. If a Notary resigns, is disqualified, is removed from office or allows a commission to expire without obtaining another commission within 30 days, then his or her notarial records must be delivered to the county clerk's office where the Notary's oath of office and bond are on file within 30 days of commission resignation, revocation or expiration.

If a Notary refuses to deliver notarial records to the county clerk as specified by law, the Notary is guilty of a misdemeanor and is liable for damages suffered by any person as a result.

If the Notary dies, the Notary's executor or personal representative must promptly notify the Secretary of State and deliver all the decedent's notarial records and papers to the county clerk's office where the Notary's oath and bond are filed.

After 10 years, the office of the county clerk may destroy the notarial records upon court order. Notaries may never destroy their notarial records (Government Code, Section 8209).

Answer Inquiries from State. Upon official written request, a Notary must send certified copies of journal entries to the Secretary of State within the time specified (Government Code, Section 8205[b][1]). (See "Certified Copies of Notarial Records," pages 32–33.)

In addition, the Notary must respond within 30 days to any request from the Secretary of State sent by certified mail for information relating to official acts performed by the Notary (Government Code, Section 8205[b][2]).

Notarial Certificate

Requirement. In notarizing any document, a Notary must complete a notarial certificate. The certificate is wording that indicates exactly what the Notary has certified. The notarial certificate may either be printed on the document itself or on an attachment. The certificate should contain:

1) A venue indicating where the notarization is performed. "State of California, County of _____," is the typical venue wording, with the county name inserted in the blank. The letters "SS." or "SCT." sometimes appear after the venue; they abbreviate the traditional Latin word *scilicet,* meaning "in particular" or "namely."

2) A statement of particulars indicating what the notarization has attested to. An acknowledgment certificate would include such wording as:

"On _____ before me, (here insert name and title of the officer), personally appeared _____, who proved to me on the basis of satisfactory evidence to be the person(s)..."

A jurat certificate would include such wording as:

"Subscribed and sworn to (or affirmed) before me on this _____ day of _____ (month), _____ (year), by _____, proved to me on the basis of satisfactory evidence to be the person(s) ... "

3) A testimonium clause, which may be optional if the date is included in the statement of particulars: "Witness my hand and official seal, this _____ day of _____ (month), ____ (year)." In this short sentence, the Notary formally attests to the truthfulness of the preceding facts in the certificate. "Hand" means signature.

4) The official signature of the Notary, exactly as the name appears on the Notary's commission.

5) The official seal of the Notary. On many certificates the letters "L.S." appear, indicating where the seal is to be located. These letters abbreviate the Latin term *locus sigilli*, meaning "place of the seal." An inking seal should be placed near but not over the letters, so that wording imprinted by the seal will not be obscured. An embossing seal, used in conjunction with an inking seal, may be placed directly over the letters — slightly displacing portions of the characters and leaving a clue that document examiners can use to distinguish an original from a forged photocopy.

Loose Certificates. When certificate wording is not preprinted on the document, a loose certificate may be attached by the Notary. This form is typically stapled to the document's left margin following the signature page.

To prevent a loose certificate from being removed and fraudulently placed on another document, there are precautions a Notary can take. The Notary can emboss the certificate and document together, writing "attached document bears embossment" on the certificate, or write a brief description of the document on the certificate: "This certificate is attached to a _____ (title or type of document), dated _____, of _____ (number) pages, signed by _____ (name[s] of signer[s])."

While fraud-deterrent steps such as these can make it much more difficult for a loose certificate to be removed and misused, there is no absolute protection against its removal and misuse. Notaries must ensure that, while a certificate remains in their control, it is attached only to the intended document.

Do Not Pre-Sign/Seal Certificates. A Notary must never sign and/or seal certificates ahead of time or permit other persons to attach loose notarial certificates to documents. Also, the Notary should not send an unattached, signed and sealed loose certificate through the mail, even if requested to do so by a signer who previously appeared before the Notary. These actions may facilitate fraud or forgery, and they could subject the Notary to lawsuits to recover damages resulting from the Notary's neglect or misconduct. In addition, the Secretary of State could fine the Notary up to $750 and revoke, suspend or refuse to renew the Notary's commission (Government Code, Section 8214.1 and Civil Code, Section 1188).

Standard Size for Certificates. Additional recording fees will be charged for documents when any page of the document, including the attached notarial certificate, is not the standard 8½ by 11-inch size. The extra fee is $3 per page and is applied to all pages of the document. The person who files the document, not the Notary, is responsible for the extra fees (Government Code, Sections 27361 and 27361.5).

False Certificate or Writing. A Notary who knowingly completes a certificate or executes a writing containing statements the Notary knows are false may be charged with a misdemeanor. A misdemeanor charge may be brought within four years after discovery of the violation, or within four years after completion of the offense, whichever is later (Government Code, Section 6203).

In addition, any Notary who knowingly completes a false acknowledgment certificate may be charged with forgery (Penal Code, Section 470).

Furthermore, a Notary may have his or her commission revoked for executing a certificate containing information the Notary knows is false and may be fined up to $1,500 (Government Code, Section 8214.1)

Finally, effective January 1, 2008, a Notary who willfully states as true any material fact that he or she knows is false may be fined up to $10,000. This penalty may be imposed by the Secretary of State in an administrative hearing or by a public prosecutor in superior court (Civil Code, Section 1189).

Notary Seal

Requirement. A California Notary must affix an impression of an official seal on the certificate portion of every document notarized (Government Code, Section 8207).

Format. The seal may be either circular and not more than two inches in diameter or rectangular and not more than an inch in height and 2½ inches in length. In either case, it must have a serrated or milled edged border (Government Code, Section 8207).

Inking and Embosser Seals. The seal must imprint or emboss a photographically reproducible impression. Because the image must be photocopiable, most Notaries use an inked rubber stamp seal, since an embossment would have to be smudged or darkened to be picked up on camera. An embosser may be used in addition to the required photographically reproducible seal, but it must not be used over the reproducible inking seal or over the Notary's signature (Government Code, Section 8207).

Required Information. The seal impression must clearly show the following information (Government Code, Section 8207):

- Name of the Notary (exactly as it appears on the commission certificate).

- The circular California state seal.

- The words "Notary Public."

- The county where the Notary's oath and bond are filed.

- The Notary's commission expiration date.

- The Notary's commission number.

- The ID number of the seal manufacturer or vendor.

Lost or Damaged Seal. Any Notary whose official seal is lost, misplaced, destroyed, broken, damaged or otherwise unworkable must immediately mail or deliver written notice to the Secretary of State, who will issue a Certificate of Authorization to obtain a replacement. Failure to report can result in a $1,500 fine (Government Code, Section 8207.3).

Security of Seal. Effective January 1, 1998, the seal must be kept in a locked and secured area under direct supervision and control of the Notary. Failure to secure the seal is reason for the Secretary of State to revoke, suspend or refuse to grant a Notary commission. In addition, a fine of up to $750 may be imposed. A Notary who willfully fails to safeguard the seal, or who surrenders the seal to any person not authorized to possess it, is guilty of a misdemeanor. A misdemeanor charge may be brought within four years after discovery of the violation, or within four years after completion of the offense, whichever is later (Government Code, Sections 8207, 8214.1, 8214.15 and 8228.1).

Certificate of Authorization. No person may purchase a California Notary seal without first presenting to the approved seal vendor a "Certificate of Authorization to Purchase a Notary Stamp," issued by the Secretary of State. This certificate is sent to each newly commissioned Notary, along with the commissioning papers (Government Code, Section 8207.2).

The seal vendor must keep a copy of each Certificate of Authorization presented and a record of each Notary's ID number. The vendor must submit the original Certificate of Authorization, containing a sample impression of the new seal, to the Secretary of State for verification of the vendor's authority to manufacture a seal and for recordkeeping (Government Code, Section 8207.3).

The failure of a Notary or vendor to comply with the procedures regarding the Certificate of Authorization can result in a $1,500 fine for each violation. Such a penalty would result from a civil lawsuit initiated by the Attorney General or a local district attorney, city attorney or prosecutor (Government Code, Section 8207.4).

Misuse of Seal. Any person who, with intent to defraud, forges or counterfeits a Notary seal to give a document the appearance of being government-issued is guilty of forgery. Documents may include, but are not limited to, an identification card, driver's license, birth certificate, passport or Social Security card. Forgery is punishable by imprisonment for up to one year (Penal Code, Sections 470, 472 and 473).

Use of Seal for Endorsement or Testimonial. Notaries may not use the official seal to endorse or promote any product, service or contest. The Notary seal may only be used to carry out the official duties of a Notary Public (Government Code, Section 8207).

Placement of Seal Impression. The Notary's official seal impression should be placed near the Notary's signature on the notarial certificate. It must be easily readable and should not be placed over signatures or any printed matter on the document. An illegible or improperly placed seal may result in rejection of the document by a recorder.

L.S. The letters "L.S." — from the Latin *locus sigilli*, meaning "location of the seal" — appear on many notarial certificates to indicate where the Notary seal should be placed. Only an embosser seal, used in addition to an inking seal, should be placed over these letters. The inking seal should be placed near but not over the letters.

Plastic Subdivision Maps. Because many seal inks smear on plastic-surfaced subdivision maps, acknowledgment certificates printed on such maps need not bear the Notary's seal if the Notary's name, county of principal place of business and commission expiration date are typed or printed below the Notary's signature (Government Code, Section 66436).

Recording Requirements. If a Notary fails to use a photographically reproducible inking seal, the document may be accepted for recording in a California county if an embossing seal is present and legible and if the Notary has printed or typed the following below or adjacent to the Notary's signature: the Notary's name, the county of the Notary's principal place of business, the Notary's telephone number, the Notary's commission number and the Notary's commission expiration date (Government Code, Section 66436).

A document bearing an impression of a Notary seal that is not sufficiently legible to produce a readable photographic record may be accepted for recording if the document is substituted with a legible original or a typewritten or handwritten copy attached to the document and accompanied by a signed declaration under penalty of perjury certifying that the substitute copy is a true copy of the original (Government Code, Section 27361.7).

Electronic Seal. Documents that now can be notarized and transmitted electronically to the recorder by a "trusted submitter" include substitutions of trustee, assignments of a deed of trust and reconveyance deeds — but no others. A trusted submitter is a title insurer; underwritten title company; institutional lender; or local, state or federal governmental entity. Notaries are permitted to notarize these electronic documents without affixing a physical Notary seal image to the form as long as the information contained in the Notary seal is included with the Notary's electronic signature (Government Code, Section 578). (See "Electronic Signatures," page 74.)

Fees for Notarial Services

Maximum Fees. The following maximum fees are authorized for California Notaries:

- Acknowledgments — $10. For taking an acknowledgment, the maximum fee is $10 for each signature notarized. For notarizing a single document with signatures of three persons appearing before the Notary, a maximum of $30 could be charged (Government Code, Section 8211).

- Certified Copy of Power of Attorney — $10. A maximum of $10 per copy may be charged by a Notary for certifying a copy of a power of attorney (Government Code, Section 8211).

- Copy of Journal Entry — 30¢. A maximum of 30 cents per photocopy may be charged for providing a photocopy of an entry in the Notary's journal (Government Code, Section 8206).

- Depositions — $20. For all services rendered in taking a deposition, the maximum fee is $20, plus $5 for administering an oath to the witness and $5 for completing the certificate on the deposition (Government Code, Section 8211).

- Immigration Papers — $10 per set. A nonattorney Notary bonded as an immigration consultant may not charge more than $10 per set of forms (apart from the standard notarial fee) for entering data provided by a client on state or federal immigration forms. Violators may be fined up to $750 (Government Code, Sections 8214.1, 8214.15 and 8223).

- <u>Jurats</u> — $10. For executing a jurat, including the administration of the oath or affirmation, the fee is not to exceed $10 per signature notarized (Government Code, Section 8211).

- <u>Oaths and Affirmations</u> — $10. For administering an oath or affirmation, with or without completion of a jurat, the maximum fee is $10 per oath (Government Code, Section 8211).

- <u>Proofs of Execution by Subscribing Witness</u> — $10. For taking a proof of execution, including the administration of the oath or affirmation, the maximum fee is the same as for an acknowledgment: $10 for each signature of the principal proven by a subscribing witness (Government Code, Section 8211).

- <u>Protests</u> — $10. For taking a protest, the maximum fee is $10. For serving a notice of nonpayment or nonacceptance, the fee is $5. For recording a protest, the fee is $5 (Government Code, Section 8211).

<u>Option Not to Charge</u>. Notaries are not required to charge for their notarial services, and they may charge any fee less than the maximum. However, Notaries employed by some public agencies may be required by their employers to charge for their services and to remit the fees to the employer (Government Code, Section 6100).

<u>Overcharging</u>. Charging more than the legally prescribed fees is reason for the Secretary of State to revoke, suspend or refuse to grant a Notary commission. In addition, a fine of up to $750 may be imposed (Government Code, Sections 8214.1 and 8214.15).

<u>Travel Fees</u>. Charges for travel by a Notary are not specified by law. Such fees are allowed only if the Notary and signer agree beforehand on the amount to be charged. The Notary should tell

the signer that a travel fee is not stated in the law and is separate from the notarial fees.

Obligation to Itemize. A Notary employed by a county or judicial district is required to make out a receipt for notarial fees for any person requesting one. The Notary is liable for three times the notarial fee for neglecting or refusing to honor such a request (Government Code, Section 6109).

Failure to Complete Notarization. For failing or refusing to complete a lawful request for notarization once payment is offered for it, a Notary is liable for any resulting ramifications (Government Code, Section 6110).

Notary/Employer Agreement. A private employer who purchases the notarial supplies and bond of an employee-Notary may make a voluntary mutual agreement with the employee-Notary to remit all notarial fees collected to the fund from which the employee-Notary is paid (Government Code, Section 8202.7).

Absentee Ballots. No fee may be charged for notarizing absentee ballots or other voting materials (Government Code, Section 8211), or a nomination document or circulator's affidavit (Election Code, Section 8080). A U.S. military veteran may not be charged for notarization of a claim for any veteran's benefit (Government Code, Section 8211).

Incomplete Documents

Do Not Notarize. California Notaries are prohibited from taking an acknowledgment or a proof of execution of any document that is not complete (Government Code, Section 8205).

Any blanks in a document should be filled in by the signer. If the blanks are inapplicable and intended to be left unfilled, the signer should be asked to line through each space (using ink) or to write "Not Applicable" or "N/A."

If there is doubt about a document's completeness, the Notary should ask the signer. If the signer says the instrument is incomplete, the Notary should refuse to notarize; if the signer says it is complete, the Notary might accept the signer's word, unless the document contains obvious blanks.

Disqualifying Interest

Financial or Beneficial Interest. A Notary may not perform any notarization related to a transaction in which that Notary has a direct financial or beneficial interest (Government Code, Section 8224).

A financial or beneficial interest exists when the Notary is named in a financial transaction or when the Notary receives, as a result of the transaction, an advantage, right, privilege, property or fee valued in excess of the lawfully prescribed notarial fee.

In regard to real estate transactions, a Notary is considered to have a disqualifying financial or beneficial interest when that Notary is a grantor or grantee, a mortgagor or mortgagee, a trustor or trustee, a vendor or vendee, a lessor or lessee or a beneficiary of the transaction.

Exemptions. Certain persons are exempt from this beneficial and financial interest provision. A Notary who is an agent, employee, insurer, attorney, escrow officer or lender for a person signing a document may notarize the document without being considered to have a disqualifying interest. For example, a real estate agent can notarize a document relating to a property transfer even if the agent derives a commission from that transaction.

Any challenged case of disqualifying financial or beneficial interest would be decided in court. Thus, it is always safest for a Notary to ensure that he or she has no financial or beneficial interest whatsoever in a transaction regardless of what the law allows (Government Code, Section 8224).

Refusal of Services

Legal Requests for Services. Notaries must honor all lawful and reasonable requests to notarize, whether or not the person requesting the act is a client or customer of the Notary or the Notary's employer. Not providing services when required to do so could cause the Notary to be liable if any damages resulted from the refusal (Government Code, Section 6110).

Exception for Employer/Notary Agreement. A Notary and employer may agree to limit the Notary's services solely to transactions directly related to the employer's business during business hours (Government Code, Section 8202.8). (See "Employer/Notary Agreement," pages 62-63.)

Reasonable Care

Responsibility. As public servants, Notaries must act responsibly and exercise reasonable care in the performance of their official duties. If a Notary fails to do so, he or she may be subject to a civil lawsuit to recover financial damages caused by his or her error or omission. In general, reasonable care is a degree of concern and attentiveness that a person of normal intelligence and responsibility would exhibit. If a Notary can show a judge or jury that he or she did everything expected of a reasonable person, the judge or jury is obligated by law to find the Notary not liable for damages.

Complying with all pertinent laws is the first rule of reasonable care for a Notary. If there are no statutory guidelines in a given instance, the Notary should use common sense and prudence. (See "Steps to Proper Notarization," pages 14–18.)

Employer/Notary Agreement

Agreement to Limit Notary's Services. A private employer who has paid for an employee-Notary's commission, bond, stamp and other supplies may limit the Notary's services during business hours solely to transactions directly related to the employer's business, if the Notary agrees (Government Code, Sections 8202.7 and 8202.8).

It may be helpful to the Notary to have this agreement in writing to prevent requests for exceptions when limiting services.

Noncustomer Discrimination Prohibited. An employer/Notary agreement does not permit discrimination between customers and noncustomers, but only between business-related and nonbusiness-related documents. A business-related document is one that the employer is either named in or acting as an agent in relation to. If a bank customer asks an employee-Notary, who has entered into such an agreement with the bank, to notarize a document that does not involve the bank, the Notary must refuse (Government Code, Section 8202.8).

Once a Notary enters into an agreement with an employer to only notarize business-related documents, the Notary may not suspend the agreement just for customers or even for colleagues, coworkers or supervisors. However, the Notary may notarize other types of documents during nonbusiness hours (Government Code, Section 8202.7).

Fees. A Notary who enters into such an agreement with a private employer may agree to hand over the notarial fees to the employer. The law requires the employer to place those fees into the account from which the Notary is paid (Government Code, Section 8202.7).

Not Applicable to Government Employees. Employer/Notary agreements do not apply to government-employee Notaries.

Notarizing a Signature by Mark

Mark Serves as Signature. A person who is unable to sign his or her name may instead use a mark — an "X" for example — as a signature, as long as there are two witnesses to the making of the mark (Civil Code, Section 14).

Witnesses. For a mark to be notarized, two witnesses to the making of the mark are required. Both witnesses must sign the document, and one witness must print legibly the marker's name beside the mark on the document (Civil Code, Section 14).

Witnesses Sign Journal. Although not a requirement of law, the National Notary Association recommends that the Notary record the names of the witnesses to a signature by mark in the journal entry for the transaction and have both witnesses sign the journal.

Witnesses' Statement. For a document to be filed in California, county recorders require the witnesses to sign a statement on the document confirming the particulars of the procedure. This statement is in addition to the notarial certificate. California county recorders prefer the following wording:

_____ (name of signer), being unable to write, made his/her mark in our presence and requested the first of the undersigned to write his/her name, which he/she did, and we now subscribe our names as witnesses thereto.

_____ (Signature of witness #1)
_____ (Signature of witness #2)

Signature-by-Mark Certificate. A properly witnessed mark is considered a valid signature under law, so no special notarial certificate is required. For acknowledgments filed in California, Notaries must use the all-purpose form; jurats require the prescribed jurat wording.

Notarizing for Minors

Under Age 18. Generally, persons must reach the age of majority before they can handle their own legal affairs and sign documents for themselves. In California, the age of majority is 18. Normally, parents or guardians will sign on a minor's behalf. In certain cases, where minors are engaged in business transactions or serving as court witnesses, they may lawfully sign documents and have their signatures notarized.

Include Age Next to Signature. When notarizing for a minor, the Notary should ask the young signer to write his or her age next to the signature to alert any person relying upon the document that the signer is a minor. The Notary is not required to verify the minor signer's age.

Identification. The method for identifying a minor is the same as that for an adult. Because minors often do not possess acceptable identification documents, such as driver's licenses or passports, determining the identity of a minor can be a problem. If the minor does not have an acceptable ID, then another form of satisfactory evidence must be used (e.g., one personally known or two unknown credible identifying witnesses). (See "Credible Identifying Witness(es)," pages 45–47.)

Authentication

Documents Sent Out of State. Documents notarized in California and sent to other states may be required to bear proof that the Notary's signature and seal are genuine and that the Notary had authority to act at the time of notarization. This process of proving the genuineness of an official signature and seal is called authentication or legalization.

In California, proof of the Notary's commission is in the form of an authenticating certificate attached to a notarized document by either the county clerk's office where the Notary's oath and bond are filed or the Secretary of State's office. These certificates are also known as certificates of authority, certificates of capacity, certificates of authenticity, certificates of prothonotary and "flags."

The fee for an authenticating certificate from the county clerk will vary from county to county. An authenticating certificate from the Secretary of State costs $20 through the mail (check made out to "Secretary of State") and takes about two weeks to process. The original notarized document, a cover letter indicating the destination of the document, and an addressed, postage-paid return envelope must be included. This should all be sent to:

> Office of Secretary of State
> Notary Public Section
> P.O. Box 942877
> Sacramento, CA 94277-0001

In person, an authenticating certificate from the California Secretary of State may be obtained at 1500 11th Street, 2nd Floor, in Sacramento. For in-person pickup and processing while you wait, the cost is $26. An appointment is not necessary. It is not the Notary's responsibility to pick up or pay for the certificate of authority. Additional information is available by calling the Secretary of State's Notary Public Section at (916) 653-3595.

Documents Sent Out of Country. If the notarized document is going outside the United States, a chain authentication process may be necessary, and additional certificates of authority may have to be obtained from the U.S. Department of State in Washington, DC, a foreign consulate in Washington, DC and a ministry of foreign affairs in the particular foreign nation.

Apostilles and the Hague Convention. More than 90 nations, including the United States, subscribe to a treaty under the auspices of the Hague Conference that simplifies authentication of notarized documents exchanged between these nations. The official name of this treaty, adopted by the Conference on October 5, 1961, is the *Hague Convention Abolishing the Requirement of Legalization for Foreign Public Documents.* (For a list of the subscribing countries, see "Hague Convention

Nations," pages 140–142.)

Under the Hague Convention, only one authenticating certificate called an *apostille* is necessary to ensure acceptance in these subscribing countries. (*Apostille* is French for "notation.")

In California, *apostilles* are issued by the Secretary of State's office. The procedure and fees are the same as for obtaining an ordinary authenticating certificate. Ensure that the country for which the document is destined is also specified.

Unauthorized Practice of Law

Do Not Assist in Legal Matters. A Notary who is not an attorney may not give legal advice or accept fees for legal advice. The nonattorney Notary may not assist a signer to draft, prepare, select, complete or understand a document or transaction. A Notary may only be responsible for the information on the notarial certificate.

Notaries may complete legal documents in which they are named as a subscribing party, but may never notarize their own signatures. Notaries involved in the unauthorized practice of law may have their commissions revoked and be criminally prosecuted (Government Code, Section 8214.1 and Business and Professions Code, Section 6125).

Exceptions. Nonattorney Notaries who are specially trained, certified or licensed in a particular field (e.g., real estate) may offer advice in that field only. Paralegals under the supervision of an attorney may give advice about documents in routine legal matters.

Advertising

False or Misleading Advertising. A Notary's commission can be revoked or suspended if the Notary uses false or misleading advertising to misrepresent the authority, rights and privileges of a Notary. In addition, a fine of up to $1,500 may be imposed (Government Code, Sections 8214.1 and 8214.15).

Foreign-Language Advertising. A nonattorney Notary advertising notarial services in a foreign language must take steps to guard against misinterpretation of his or her function as a Notary. Nonattorney Notaries are required to include in any such foreign-language advertisement the following, in both English and the foreign language (Government Code, Section 8219.5):

1) The statement: "I am not an attorney and, therefore, cannot give legal advice about immigration or any other legal matters."

2) The fees that a Notary is allowed to charge.

These requirements apply to signs and all other forms of written communication (business cards, telephone book ads) with the exception of a single desk plaque. Furthermore, literal translation of "Notary Public" into Spanish (*Notario Publico*) is prohibited by law. For violations, a Notary's commission can be suspended for a year or revoked. On the second offense, it must be revoked permanently (Government Code, Section 8219.5 and Business and Professions Code, Section 22442.3).

Immigration Expert. No person who claims to be an immigration expert or counselor may also advertise as a Notary Public. This provision attempts to prevent immigration counselors from misrepresenting their authority. Violators may be fined up to $1,500 (Government Code, Section 8223).

Foreign Languages

Foreign-Language Documents. California Notaries are not expressly prohibited from notarizing a non-English document. However, the notarial certificate and document signature should be in English or in a language the Notary can read.

There are difficulties to consider with foreign-language documents: A blatant fraud might be undetectable, the U.S. Notary seal might be misinterpreted in another country and making a complete journal entry might be difficult.

Foreign-Language Signers. There should always be direct communication between the Notary and document signer, whether in English or another language. The Notary should never rely upon an intermediary or interpreter to determine a signer's willingness or competence. A third party may have reasons to misrepresent the transaction to the Notary and/or to the signer.

Immigration

Documents. Certain immigration documents may be notarized, such as the Affidavit of Support (I-134). However, state law places certain restrictions on the Notary in the area of immigration. Notaries must strictly adhere to these laws.

A nonattorney Notary who is also bonded as an immigration consultant may enter data provided by a client on state or federal immigration forms. Notaries who enter data in immigration forms without also being bonded as an immigration consultant may be fined up to $750 (Government Code, Sections 8214.1, 8214.15 and 8223).

Advertising. No person who claims to be an immigration expert or counselor may also advertise as a Notary Public. This provision is designed to prevent immigration counselors from misrepresenting their powers to unsuspecting foreigners. Violators may have their Notary commissions revoked or suspended or be fined up to $1,500 (Government Code, Sections 8214.1, 8214.15 and 8223 and Business and Professions Code, Section 22442.3).

Identifying Signers. In notarizing forms that will be submitted to the U.S. Citizenship and Immigration Services (USCIS), a Notary may accept as proof of identity any ID or documentation acceptable to the USCIS (Government Code, Section 8230).

Naturalization Certificates. A Notary may only photocopy a certificate of naturalization for lawful purposes. The NNA recommends a Notary only certify a copy of the certificate if written directions are provided by a U.S. immigration authority.

False Statement on Immigration Document. It is misdemeanor for any person (including a Notary) to knowingly, and for payment, make a false statement on a document related to immigration. The person may be imprisoned in a county jail for a maximum of six months, be fined up to $2,500, or both (Penal Code, Section 653.55).

Military-Base Notaries
Qualifications. The Secretary of State may appoint Notaries for military bases of the U.S. Army, Navy, Coast Guard, Air Force and Marine Corps in the state. These military-base Notaries must (Government Code, Sections 8203.1 to 8203.3):

1) Be citizens of the United States.

2) Be at least 18 years old.

3) Have successfully completed the Notary examination.

4) Be federal civil service employees at the base where they will act.

5) Receive the recommendation of the base commanding officer.

6) Effective July 1, 2005 have completed a state-approved education course on the Notary's duties and functions.

Term of Office. The military-base Notary is commissioned for four years. However, this person ceases to be a Notary whenever he or she ceases to be employed as a civil service employee at the base where appointed. The commanding officer must notify the Secretary of State within 30 days of termination of the Notary's employment (Government Code, Section 8203.4).

Jurisdiction. Military-base Notaries can notarize only at the base where they were appointed (Government Code, Section 8203.2).

Fees. Military-base Notaries may not charge for notarial services (Government Code, Section 8203.6).

Certificates. On notarial certificates, military-base Notaries must include the name of the base where the document was notarized (Government Code, Section 8203.5).

Military Officer Notarizations

May Notarize Worldwide. Certain U.S. military officers may notarize for military personnel and their dependents anywhere in the world. Under statutory authority, the following persons are authorized to act as Notaries (Civil Code, Section 1183.5):

- Civilian attorneys employed as legal assistance attorneys and licensed to practice law in the United States.

- Judge advocates on active duty or training as reservists on inactive duty.

- All adjutants, assistant adjutants, acting adjutants and personnel adjutants.

- Enlisted paralegals, personnel rank E-4 or higher, on active duty or training on inactive duty.

- Active duty personnel who are commissioned officers or senior noncommissioned officers (rank E-7 or higher) who are stationed at a Geographically Separated Unit (GSU) or location where no authorized Notary official is available, and who are appointed in writing by the unit's servicing general court-martial convening authority.

Certificate. When signing documents in their official capacity, military-officer Notaries must specify the date and location of the notarization and their title and office and must use a raised seal or inked stamp citing Title 10 U.S.C. 1044a (U.S. Code, Title 10, Sections 936, 1044a).

Authentication. Authentication of a military-officer notarization certificate is not required.

Wills

Do Not Offer Advice. Often, people attempt to draw up wills without benefit of legal counsel and then bring these homemade testaments to a Notary to have them "legalized," expecting the Notary to know how to proceed. In advising or assisting such persons, the Notary risks prosecution for the unauthorized practice of law and the Notary's ill-informed advice may do considerable damage to the affairs of the signer.

Wills are highly sensitive documents, the format of which is dictated by strict laws. The slightest deviation from these laws can nullify a will. In some cases, holographic (handwritten) wills have actually been voided by notarization.

Do Not Proceed Without Certificate Wording. A Notary may notarize a will if the would-be testator is following the advice of an attorney, but only if notarial wording is provided. The Notary cannot advise the signer on how to proceed. Wills probated in California generally do not require notarization, though they must be witnessed. However, a California Notary may be asked to notarize a will that will be probated in another state.

Living Wills. Documents popularly called living wills may be notarized. These are not actual wills; they are a form of advance health care directive, in which the signer gives instructions for medial treatment in the event that he or she becomes unable to personally provide such instructions due to illness or incapacity.

Durable Power of Attorney for Health Care

Health Care Proxy. A durable power of attorney for health care is another form of advance health care directive. This type of directive differs from a living will in that it appoints a specific person to make decisions on behalf of a principal (the signer) in the event that the principal becomes unable to do so due to illness or incapacity.

Signing Requirements. To be legally valid, a durable power of attorney for health care must contain the date of signing and must be signed either by the principal or (if the principal cannot sign) in the principal's name by another adult in the principal's presence and under his or her direction. The power of attorney must be either acknowledged before a Notary or signed by two witnesses.

Notarization. Effective January 1, 2008, if the principal chooses to acknowledge the power of attorney before a Notary, then the principal must leave his or her right thumbprint in the Notary's journal.

Witness Requirements. If witnesses are used, they must be adults, must witness the signing or acknowledgment of the instrument and must sign a witness's statement as prescribed by Probate Code Section 4701.

At least one witness must be a person who is not related to the principal by blood, marriage or adoption and does not have an interest in the principal's estate.

In addition, the following persons may not act as a witness (Probate Code, Sections 4122 and 4701):

- The principal's attorney in fact

- The principal's health care provider or an employee of that health care provider

- The operator or an employee of a community or residential care facility

Skilled Nursing Facility. If a durable power of attorney is executed by a patient in a skilled nursing facility, a patient advocate or ombudsman must sign either as one of the two required witnesses, or in addition to the notarization. The patient advocate or ombudsman must delare that he or she is serving as a witness in accordance with the provisions of Probate Code, Section 4675 (Probate Code, Section 4701).

A "skilled nursing facility" is defined in the California Health and Safety Code, Section 1250(a)(2)(c) as "a health facility that provides skilled nursing care and supportive care to patients whose primary need is for availability of skilled nursing care on an extended basis."

Electronic Power of Attorney for Health Care. An electronic durable power of attorney for health care is legally valid if it meets the same requirements as a written power of attorney. However, the electronic instrument must be acknowledged by the principal before a Notary Public; two witnesses may not be used instead (Probate Code, Section 4673).

The electronic durable power of attorney for health care would be signed with an electronic signature by both the principal and the Notary. (See "Electronic Signatures," page 74.) While any type of electronic signature technology may be used, Probate Code Section 4673 prescribes certain rules for digital signatures. (See "Digital Signatures," page 74.)

If a digital signature is used in executing the power of attorney, it must:

- Meet the requirements of Government Code Section 16.5 and Chapter 10 of Division 7 of Title 2 of the California Code of Regulations or use an algorithm approved by the National Institute of Standards and Technology.

- Be unique to the person using it.

- Be under the exclusive control of the individual using it.

- Be linked to the data in such a way that if the data are changed, the signature is invalidated.

- Persist with the electronic document and not by association in separate files.

- Be bound to a digital certificate.

Effective January 1, 2008, the principal electronically signing a durable power of attorney for health care must leave his or her right thumb in the Notary's journal.

Confidential Marriage Certificates

Restrictions. Only specially screened Notaries may issue and notarize confidential marriage certificates. To receive such authorization, a Notary must file an application and a $300 annual fee with the county clerk of the county in which the Notary lives.

After an applicant has undergone a background check and a two-hour course of instruction, the county clerk may issue an authorization for the Notary to execute these certificates. This authorization requires annual renewal (Family Code, Sections 530–536).

Certificates and Fees. Blank confidential marriage certificates are provided to authorized Notaries by the county clerk for a fee, which the Notary may charge to the married couple along with the notarial fee for a jurat (Family Code, Section 503).

Cannot Perform Marriages. Although a California Notary may issue and notarize confidential marriage certificates, the Notary cannot perform the actual marriage ceremony unless he or she is a religious or civil official authorized to solemnize marriages.

Common Interest Development Elections

Authority. Effective July 1, 2006, Notaries are authorized as an independent third party to inspect and guarantee the integrity of a homeowner's association election, provided the Notary is not: a member of, or candidate for, the board of directors; related to a member of, or candidate for, the board of directors; or currently employed or under contract to the association for paid services, unless expressly authorized by the rules of the association (Civil Code, Section 1363.03).

Electronic Signatures

Recognized by State. California's Uniform Electronic Transactions Act (UETA) recognizes that electronic signatures may be used with the same legal effect as pen-and-ink signatures, and also recognizes their use by Notaries in performing electronic notarial acts (Civil Code, Section 1633.11).

Digital Signatures. A digital signature is a particular kind of electronic signature created through "public key cryptography," with the following attributes (Government Code, Section 16.5):

- Unique to the person using it

- Capable of verification

- Under the sole control of the person using it

- Linked to data in such a manner that if the data is changed, the digital signature is invalidated

Electronic Real Property Documents. Beginning September 21, 2004, certain "digital documents" — documents created, generated, signed, notarized and transmitted electronically — will require signing parties and Notaries to use electronic signatures to execute these forms. Under law, Notaries may notarize digital reconveyance instruments, substitutions of trustee and assignments of deeds of trust without affixing a physical notarial seal image to the form, as long as the information contained in the notarial seal is included with the Notary's electronic signature. After the notarization is complete, the digital document may be electronically recorded in any California county if the county's electronic recording system has been certified by the Attorney General (Government Code, Section 27391).

MISCONDUCT, FINES AND PENALTIES

Misconduct

Application Misstatement. Substantial and material misstatement or omission in the application for a Notary commission is reason for the Secretary of State to revoke, suspend or refuse to grant a Notary commission (Government Code, Section 8214.1).

<u>Felony Conviction</u>. Conviction for a felony or any offense involving moral turpitude or of a nature incompatible with notarial duties, such as forgery, is reason for the Secretary of State to revoke, suspend or refuse to grant a Notary commission. Pleading *nolo contendere* (no contest) is considered a conviction (Government Code, Section 8214.1).

<u>Professional Misconduct</u>. Revocation, suspension, restriction or denial of a professional license for misconduct, dishonesty or any cause substantially relating to notarial duties or responsibilities is reason for the Secretary of State to revoke, suspend or refuse to grant a Notary commission (Government Code, Section 8214.1).

<u>Failure of Duty</u>. Failure to fully and faithfully discharge the duties or responsibilities of a Notary, such as failing to keep a journal of notarial acts, is reason for the Secretary of State to refuse to grant or to revoke or suspend a Notary commission. In addition, a fine of up to $750 may be imposed (Government Code, Sections 8214.1 and 8214.15).

<u>Falsely Acting as a Notary</u>. Any person not commissioned as a Notary who represents him- or herself, advertises or acts like a Notary is guilty of a misdemeanor (Government Code, Section 8227.1).

Any non-Notary who represents him- or herself as a Notary in relation to any document affecting title to, or placing an encumbrance or interest secured by a mortgage or trust deed on, real property of certain single-family residences, is guilty of a felony and may have an application for a Notary commission denied or a commission suspended or revoked (Government Code, Section 8227.3).

<u>Making False Statements to Notary</u>. Any person who knowingly makes a false sworn statement to a Notary, to induce the Notary to perform improper notarizations with regard to the type of real property documents described above, is guilty of a felony and may have an application for a Notary commission denied or a commission suspended or revoked (Government Code, Section 8214.1[b] and Penal Code, Section 115.5[b]).

False or Misleading Advertising. The use of false or misleading advertising by a Notary to represent that he or she has duties, rights and privileges not given by law may subject the Notary to a $1,500 civil penalty and is reason for the Secretary of State to revoke, suspend or refuse to grant a Notary commission (Government Code, Sections 8214.1 and 8214.15).

Improper Foreign-Language Advertising. For failing to include in the advertisement, in English and the foreign language, the statement, "I am not an attorney and, therefore, cannot give legal advice about immigration or any other legal matters," for not including the fees a Notary is allowed to charge or for including a literal Spanish translation of the words "Notary Public" (*Notario Publico* or *Notaria Publica*), a Notary's commission may be revoked or suspended for one year. On the second offense, it must be revoked permanently. In addition, a $1,500 civil penalty may be imposed (Government Code, Sections 8214.1, 8214.15 and 8219.5 and Business and Professions Code, Section 22442.3).

Advertising as Immigration Expert. No person who claims to be an immigration expert or counselor may also advertise as a Notary Public. This provision is designed to prevent immigration counselors from misrepresenting their powers to unsuspecting foreigners. Violation of the law relating to immigration matters and advertising is reason for the Secretary of State to revoke, suspend or refuse to grant a Notary commission and subjects the Notary to a $1,500 civil penalty (Government Code, Sections 8214.1, 8214.15 and 8223 and Business and Professions Code, Section 22442.3).

Acting as Immigration Consultant without Bond. A Notary may have a commission denied, suspended and revoked and be liable for a $1,500 civil penalty for entering data onto an immigration form or otherwise acting as an immigration consultant without being qualified and bonded as an immigration consultant (Government Code, Sections 8214.1 and 8223).

Unauthorized Practice of Law. The unauthorized practice of law — giving advice on legal matters when one is not a lawyer — is reason for the Secretary of State to deny, revoke or suspend a Notary's commission (Government Code, Section 8214.1 and Business and Professions Code, Section 6125).

Overcharging. Charging more than the maximum fees is reason for the Secretary of State to revoke, suspend or refuse to grant a Notary commission. In addition, a fine of up to $750 may be imposed (Government Code, Sections 8214.1 and 8214.15).

A Notary who charges more than $10 per individual for a set of forms for entering data on immigration forms at the direction of a client may be fined up to $1,500 and have his or her commission denied, suspended or revoked (Government Code, Sections 8214.1, 8214.15 and 8223).

Dishonesty or Fraud. Committing an act involving dishonesty, fraud or deceit with the intent to substantially benefit the Notary or another, or to substantially injure another, is reason for the Secretary of State to revoke, suspend or refuse to grant a Notary commission. In addition, a fine of up to $1,500 may be imposed (Government Code, Sections 8214.1 and 8214.15).

Intent to Defraud — Real Property. Any Notary who knowingly and willfully performs a notarial act with intent to defraud in relation to a deed of trust on real property (no more than four dwelling units), with knowledge that the deed contains false information or is forged, is guilty of a felony. Committing this offense also is grounds for the Secretary of State to deny, suspend or revoke the Notary's commission (Government Code, Sections 8214.1[b] and 8214.2).

Recording False Instruments. Commission denial, revocation or suspension may occur to anyone who knowingly procures or offers any false or forged instruments to be filed, registered or recorded in any public office in California that, if genuine, might be filed or recorded. Furthermore, any person who knowingly records a false or forged document for real property as described above, in addition to other penalties, may be fined up to $75,000 (Government Code, Section 8214.1 and Penal Code, Section 115 and 115.5).

Found Liable for Fraud. Being found guilty of fraud, misrepresentation or violation of state laws, and being ordered to pay damages, is reason for the Secretary of State to revoke, suspend or deny a Notary's commission (Government Code, Section 8214.1).

Incomplete Acknowledgment. Failure to complete an acknowledgment at the same time the Notary signs and seals a document is reason for the Secretary of State to revoke, suspend or refuse to grant a Notary commission. In addition, a fine of up to $750 may be imposed (Government Code, Sections 8214.1 and 8214.15).

False Certificate or Writing. A Notary who knowingly completes a certificate or executes a writing containing statements the Notary knows are false may be charged with a misdemeanor. A misdemeanor charge may be brought within four years after discovery of the violation, or within four years after completion of the offense, whichever is later (Government Code, Section 6203).

In addition, any Notary who knowingly completes a false acknowledgment certificate may be charged with forgery (Penal Code, Section 470).

Furthermore, a Notary may have his or her commission revoked for executing a certificate containing information the Notary knows is false and may be fined up to $1,500 (Government Code, Section 8214.1)

Finally, effective January 1, 2008, a Notary who willfully states as true any material fact that he or she knows is false may be fined up to $10,000. This penalty may be imposed by the Secretary of State in an administrative hearing or by a public prosecutor in superior court (Civil Code, Section 1189).

Misuse of Personal Information. The Secretary of State may deny an application or suspend or revoke the commission of a Notary who willfully and unlawfully obtains, retains, sells or uses the personal identifying information of another person to obtain goods or services; commits a crime; or commits mail theft as defined under Penal Code Section 530.5 (Government Code, Section 8214.1).

Failure to Report Loss or Theft of Journal. Willful failure on the part of a Notary to report the loss or theft of his or her journal is reason for the Secretary of State to refuse to grant, revoke or suspend a Notary commission (Government Code, Section 8214.1).

Grand Theft. Committing grand theft as defined under Penal Code Section 487 is grounds for the Secretary of State to refuse to grant, revoke or suspend a Notary commission (Government Code, Section 8214.1).

Unlawful Influence. Soliciting, coercing or influencing a Notary to perform an improper notarial act, knowing the act to be improper, is punishable as a misdemeanor and is grounds for the Secretary of State to deny, revoke or suspend a Notary commission.

Failure to Provide Journal Access. Willful failure to provide journal access to a peace officer, as defined under Penal Code Sections 830.1, 830.2 and 830.3, is grounds for the Secretary of State to refuse to grant, revoke or suspend a Notary commission. In addition, the Notary may be subject to a $2,500 civil penalty. This penalty may be brought by the Secretary of State in an administrative hearing or by a public prosecutor in superior court (Government Code, Sections 8214.1 and 8214.21).

Failure to Obtain ID for Credible Witness. If a Notary fails to require a personally-known credible identifying witness to produce a state-approved ID document, the Notary may incur a civil penalty of up to $10,000. This penalty may be brought by the Secretary of State in an administrative hearing or by a public prosecutor in superior court (Civil Code, Section 1185[b][1][B]).

Failure to Obtain Journal Thumbprint. A Notary who fails to obtain a thumbprint in the journal for a deed, quitclaim deed or deed of trust affecting real property, or for any power of attorney document, may be fined up to $2,500. The fine may be brought by the Secretary of State in an administrative hearing or by a public prosecutor in superior court (Government Code, Section 8214.23).

False Certificate on Immigration Document. It is a misdemeanor for any person, knowingly and for payment, to make a false statement on a document related to immigration. The punishment may be imprisonment in the county jail for a maximum of six months, a fine not exceeding $2,500 or both (Penal Code, Section 653.55).

Naturalization Certificate Copies or Notarizations. The law imposes harsh penalties for printing or photographing a certificate of naturalization without lawful authority. The NNA recommends a Notary only certify a copy of a certificate of naturalization if written directions are provided by a U.S. immigration authority.

Oath or Affirmation Not Administered. Failure to administer any oath or affirmation as required by law is reason for the Secretary of State to revoke, suspend or refuse to grant a Notary commission. In addition, a fine of up to $750 may be imposed (Government Code, Sections 8214.1 and 8214.15).

Journal Not Delivered. If a Notary fails or refuses to deliver notarial records to the county clerk, the Notary is guilty of a misdemeanor and is liable for damages suffered by any person as a result (Government Code, Section 8209).

Failure to Secure Journal or Seal. A Notary's failure to keep the official journal and seal in a locked and secured area may result in revocation or suspension of the Notary's commission (Government Code, Section 8214.1).

Misuse of Signature, Seal or Acknowledgment. Any person who, with intent to defraud, forges or counterfeits a Notary signature, seal or acknowledgment of a Notary, or issues an acknowledgment known by the Notary to be false is guilty of forgery, which is punishable by imprisonment for up to one year (Penal Code, Sections 470, 472 and 473).

Use of Seal for Endorsement or Testimonial. The notarial seal may only be used to carry out the official duties of a Notary Public. Notaries may not use the official seal to endorse or promote any product, service or contest (Government Code, Section 8207).

Failure to Report a Lost or Damaged Seal. Failure to report that a seal is lost, misplaced, destroyed, broken, damaged or otherwise unworkable can result in a $1,500 fine (Government Code, Sections 8207.3 and 8207.4).

Certificate of Authorization Procedure Violation. The failure of a Notary or vendor to comply with procedures regarding the Certificate of Authorization in purchasing or selling a Notary seal can result in a $1,500 fine for each violation. Such a penalty would result from a civil lawsuit initiated by the state attorney general or a local district attorney, city attorney or prosecutor (Government Code, Sections 8207.2, 8207.3 and 8207.4).

Nonpayment of Judgment. Failure to submit any remittance to the Secretary of State or to satisfy any court-ordered money judgment, including restitution, is reason for the Secretary of State to revoke, suspend or refuse to grant a Notary commission (Government Code, Section 8214.1).

Delinquency on Child Support Payments. The Secretary of State is prohibited from issuing or renewing a Notary commission for any person who has not complied with child support orders. Any commission fees that have been paid by the applicant will not be refunded (Welfare and Institutions Code, Section 11350.6).

Dishonored Check. The Secretary of State may cancel the commission of a Notary Public if any of the commission fees are not paid due to a returned check. Upon receiving notice from a financial institution that the check or draft was not honored, the Secretary of State will give written notice to the applicant requesting payment by cashier's check. Should the Secretary of State need to issue a second notice, the commission will be cancelled effective the date of that second notice (Government Code, Section 8204.1).

Violating State-Approved Education Requirements. Effective January 1, 2005, any person who provides Notary education and violates any regulations the Secretary of State adopts is subject to a maximum $1,000 fine and other appropriate damages (Government Code, Section 8201.2).

Willful Failure Regarding Journal and Seal. A Notary who willfully fails to properly maintain a journal of official acts, keep the seal under his or her direct and exclusive control or who surrenders the seal to any person not authorized to possess it, is guilty of a misdemeanor. A violation may be prosecuted within four years after discovery of the offense or within four years after completion of the offense, whichever is later (Government Code, Section 8228.1).

Criminal Conviction. Upon conviction for any criminal offense for notarial misconduct, or for any felony, in addition to any other penalty levied, a Notary's commission will be revoked by the court. The Notary must surrender his or her seal of office to the court, who will forward it, along with a certified copy of the judgment of conviction, to the Secretary of State (Government Code, Section 8214.8).

Statute of Limitations

Civil Actions. An action against a Notary's bond or the Notary, while acting in his or her official capacity, must commence within three years from performance of the act.

In cases of misfeasance and malfeasance, an action may commence within three years from performance of the act or within one year of discovery of the act. "Malfeasance" means a wrongful act performed by a public official. An example would be notarizing after the commission had expired. "Misfeasance" means a lawful act performed in an unlawful manner. An example would be performing a notarization (lawful act) without the signer present (in an unlawful manner).

However, an action must be finally brought within six years in cases when malfeasance or misfeasance by the Notary is the grounds for the lawsuit (Code of Civil Procedure, Section 338[f]).

Certain Criminal Acts. Effective January 1, 2008, the following criminal offenses may be prosecuted within four years after discovery of the offense, or within four years after completion of the offense, whichever is later:

- Making or delivering as true any certificate or writing containing statements known by the Notary to be false (Government Code, Section 6203)

- Failing to obtain a journal thumbprint for the documents for which such thumbprint is required by law (Government Code, Section 8214.23)

- Knowingly destroying, defacing or concealing any records or papers belonging to a Notary (Government Code, Section 8221)

- Improperly soliciting, influencing or coercing a Notary to perform an improper notarial act (Government Code, Section 8225)

- Failing to perform any duty in Government Code 8206 related to the Notary's seal, willfully failing to keep the seal under the Notary's exclusive control or surrendering the seal to any person not otherwise authorized by law to possess the seal (Government Code, Section 8228.1)

Right to a Hearing

Revocation, Suspension or Denial. Before a commission can be revoked or suspended, or after a commission is denied, the Notary or applicant has the right to a hearing. There is one exception, however. When it has been established within one year prior to application for renewal of a Notary's commission that the Notary has committed acts that would result in commission suspension or revocation, the Notary has no right to a hearing (Government Code, Section 8214.3).

Resignation Will Not Stop Investigation. If a Notary under investigation should resign or let his or her commission expire, the Secretary of State may still press the investigation and/or disciplinary proceedings. A record will then be made indicating whether the findings would have caused commission suspension or revocation (Government Code, Section 8214.4).

Filed with County Clerk. When a Notary's commission is revoked, a copy of the revocation is filed by the Secretary of State with the county clerk of the county where the Notary has filed an oath and bond. The county clerk then notes the revocation and the revocation date in the clerk's official records (Government Code, Section 8214.5). ■

Test Your Knowledge

Trial Exam

Instructions. This examination is designed to test your knowledge of the basic concepts of notarization. It will also help you prepare for the proctored California Notary Public exam that you must pass before being commissioned as a California Notary. The questions here, of course, are not the same as those on the official test. Also, the Notary Public exam is made up of 30 multiple-choice questions, with no true/false or essay questions as in this trial exam.

Work through this trial exam without looking at the answers provided at the end of the exam, then check your responses and note where you need additional study. Careful review of "Notary Laws Explained" (pages 19–83), the reprinted Notary statutes (pages 91–130), "10 Most-Asked Questions" (pages 9–13) and "Steps to Proper Notarization" (pages 14–18) will produce the answers.

A perfect score on this examination is 100 points. There are:

- 20 true/false questions worth 1 point each.
- 5 multiple-choice questions worth 4 points each.
- 5 fill-in-the-blank questions worth 4 points each.
- 5 essay questions worth 8 points each.

Now, get a separate sheet of paper and a pen or pencil, and get ready to test your knowledge.

True/False. For the following statements, answer true or false. Each correct answer is worth 1 point:

1. Notaries may act only in the county where they are commissioned. True or false?

2. The maximum Notary fee for taking the acknowledgment of three signers is $15. True or false?

3. It is a Notary's duty to serve all persons requesting lawful notarial acts, even those who are not customers. True or false?

4. Notaries must keep a photocopy of every document notarized. True or false?

5. A deposition is oral testimony that is written down and used as evidence in a court proceeding. True or false?

6. Notaries can withhold their services if they believe a signer is unable to understand a document. True or false?

7. It is a Notary's duty to draft powers of attorney, mortgages and deeds upon request. True or false?

8. The letters "L.S." stand for the Latin words *locus sigilli*, which mean "location of the seal." True or false?

9. Holographic wills must be notarized to be valid. True or false?

10. A Notary may rely upon two strangers as credible identifying witnesses as long as both witnesses have acceptable photo IDs. True or false?

11. A Notary can notarize documents that he or she will be signing as a corporate officer. True or false?

12. A signer of a homestead agreement for property in California must leave a right thumbprint in the Notary's journal. True or false?

13. The Notary need not reimburse the surety company for bond funds paid out to a person financially harmed by the Notary's actions. True or false?

14. A Notary is not required to determine whether a signer has the authority to sign as a corporate officer.
True or false?

15. A Notary's seal and journal belong to the Notary's employer if the employer paid for them. True or false?

16. The all-purpose certificate is not to be used for jurats or proofs of execution by subscribing witness. True or false?

17. An affirmation is the legal equivalent of an oath, but has no reference to a Supreme Being. True or false?

18. Extra recording fees are imposed on loose Notary certificates that are not exactly 8½ by 11 inches in size. True or false?

19. Notaries may not refuse to notarize blank or incomplete documents if they are signed in the Notary's presence. True or false?

20. A nonattorney Notary may not charge more than $10 for entering data in a person's immigration application. True or false?

Multiple Choice. Choose the one best answer to each question. Each correct answer is worth 4 points.

1. A Notary has a disqualifying interest when acting as ...
    a. An attorney who has drafted papers for a client.
    b. A real estate agent selling a condominium.
    c. A mortgagor in a real estate transaction.

2. To become a Notary, an applicant must ...
    a. Have been a state resident for at least one year.
    b. Be fingerprinted and report all convictions.
    c. Pass an oral exam given by the Governor's office.

3. A certificate of authority for a Notary may be obtained ...
   a. From the Governor's office or the county clerk.
   b. From a stationery store or the Notary him- or herself.
   c. From the Secretary of State or the county clerk.

4. "Satisfactory evidence" of identity means reliance on ...
   a. ID cards or credible identifying witness(es).
   b. ID cards or personal knowledge of identity.
   c. Credible identifying witness(es) or personal knowledge.

5. A California Notary may ...
   a. Take depositions and affidavits.
   b. Advertise that he or she is an immigration consultant.
   c. Certify a copy of a foreign birth certificate.

Fill in the Blank. Write in the word or phrase that best completes each sentence. Each correct answer is worth 4 points.

1. The Notary and the Notary's _____ are liable for the Notary's neglect or official misconduct.

2. A solemn, spoken pledge that is not an affirmation is called a(n) _____.

3. An acceptable ID card should contain a signature, a description and a(n) _____ of its bearer.

4. A certified copy certifies the _____ of the reproduction.

5. Wills written entirely in the testator's own handwriting are called _____.

Essay. Reply to each question or statement with a short paragraph. Each complete and correct response is worth 8 points.

1. Discuss the distinctions between a Notary bond and Notary errors and omissions insurance.

2. How does a proof of execution by subscribing witness work?

3. What is an apostille and when is it used?

4. Why should a Notary always complete the journal entry before filling out a notarial certificate?

5. Outline the differences between an acknowledgment certificate and a jurat.

Test Answers

True/False. 1. F; 2. F; 3. T; 4. F; 5. T; 6. T; 7. F; 8. T; 9. F; 10. T; 11. F; 12. F; 13. F; 14. T; 15. F; 16. T; 17. T; 18. T; 19. F; 20. T

Multiple Choice. 1. c; 2. b; 3. c; 4. a; 5. a

Fill in the Blank. 1. Surety; 2. Oath; 3. Photograph; 4. Accuracy; 5. Holographic

Essay. Responses should include the basic information in the paragraphs below:

1. A Notary bond, obtained through a state-licensed surety company, provides protection for the public in case of the Notary's negligence or intentional misconduct. Up to the cash limit of the bond, the surety agrees to pay damages to anyone who suffers a loss because of the Notary's actions; the Notary, however, must then reimburse the surety. Notary errors and omissions insurance, also purchased from a state-licensed company, protects the Notary in case of an unintentional error, up to the policy limit. The Notary does not reimburse the insurance company. A bond is required by law; errors and omissions insurance is not.

2. A proof of execution in lieu of an acknowledgment is sometimes resorted to when a document's principal signer does not appear before a Notary. In most cases, the principal will be out of town, out of state or even out of the country. A so-called subscribing witness, who has either seen the principal sign the document or taken the principal's acknowledgment of the signature, may present this document to a Notary on the principal's behalf. The

Notary must identify the subscribing witness based on the oath or affirmation of one personally known credible identifying witness, who must present an acceptable ID to the Notary. The witness must sign ("subscribe") the document in addition to the principal. The Notary then administers and oath or affirmation to the subscribing witness. A person who is a grantee or beneficiary of a document should not serve as a subscribing witness. In California, proofs of execution by subscribing witness may not be used with grant deeds, deeds of trust, quitclaim deeds, mortgages and security agreements.

3. An *apostille* is a certificate authenticating the signature and seal of a Notary. It is issued under provisions of an international treaty, signed by more than 90 nations, called the *Hague Convention Abolishing the Requirement of Legalization for Foreign Public Documents.* For notarized documents exchanged between the subscribing nations, this treaty streamlines the time-consuming authentication process known as "chain certification" by requiring only one authenticating certificate, the *apostille* (French for "notation"). *Apostilles* for California Notaries are issued by the Secretary of State.

4. Filling out a journal entry before completing a notarial certificate prevents a signer from leaving with the document before the required record of the notarization is made in the journal.

5. An acknowledgment certificate certifies that the signer of the document personally appeared before the Notary on the date and in the county indicated. It also certifies that the signer's identity was satisfactorily proven to the Notary and that the signer acknowledged having signed freely. A jurat certifies that the person signing the document did so in the Notary's presence, that the person appeared before the Notary on the date and in the county indicated, that the signer's identity was satisfactorily proven to the Notary, and that the Notary administered an oath or affirmation to the signer.

Tally Your Score

After checking your answers, add up your score. Then look at the grading scale below to determine how you stand:

- 90–100: Excellent!
- 80–89: Good, but some review needed.
- 70–79: Fair. Reread the parts of the *Primer* covering the answers that you missed.
- Below 70: Below par. Study the laws thoroughly again. ∎

California Laws Pertaining to Notaries Public

Reprinted on the following pages are pertinent sections of California statutes affecting Notaries and notarial acts, mostly drawn from the California Government Code and Civil Code.

CALIFORNIA STATUTES

GOVERNMENT CODE

§ 16.5. (a) In any written communication with a public entity, as defined in Section 811.2, in which a signature is required or used, any party to the communication may affix a signature by use of a digital signature that complies with the requirements of this section. The use of a digital signature shall have the same force and effect as the use of a manual signature if and only if it embodies all of the following attributes:

(1) It is unique to the person using it.

(2) It is capable of verification.

(3) It is under the sole control of the person using it.

(4) It is linked to data in such a manner that if the data are changed, the digital signature is invalidated.

(5) It conforms to regulations adopted by the Secretary of State. Initial regulations shall be adopted no later than January 1, 1997. In developing these regulations, the secretary shall seek the advice of public and private entities, including, but not limited to, the Department of Information Technology, the California Environmental Protection Agency, and the Department of General Services. Before the secretary adopts the regulations, he or she shall hold at least one public hearing to receive comments.

(b) The use or acceptance of a digital signature shall be at the option of the parties. Nothing in this section shall require a public entity to use or permit the use of a digital signature.

(c) Digital signatures employed pursuant to Section 71066 of the Public Resources Code are exempted from this section.

(d) "Digital signature" means an electronic identifier, created by computer, intended by the party using it to have the same force and effect as the use of a manual signature.

30. Officers of the state, or of a county or judicial district, shall not perform any official services unless upon the payment of the fees prescribed by law for the performance of the services, except as provided in this chapter.

This section shall not be construed to prohibit any notary public, except a notary public whose fees are required by law to be remitted to the state or any other public agency, from performing notarial services without charging a fee.

§ 6107. (a) No public entity, including the state, a county, city, or other political subdivision, nor any officer or employee thereof, including notaries public, shall demand or receive any fee or compensation for doing any of the following:

(1) Recording, indexing, or issuing certified copies of any discharge, certificate of service, certificate of satisfactory service, notice of separation, or report of separation of any member of the armed forces of the United States.

(2) Furnishing a certified copy of, or searching for, any public record that is to be used in an application or claim for a pension, allotment, allowance, compensation, insurance (including automatic insurance), or any other benefits under any act of Congress for service in the Armed Forces of the United States or under any law of this state relating to veterans' benefits.

(3) Furnishing a certified copy of, or searching for, any public record that is required by the Veterans Administration to be used in determining the eligibility of any person to participate in benefits made available by the Veterans Administration.

(4) Rendering any other service in connection with an application or claim referred to in paragraph (2) or (3).

(b) A certified copy of any record referred to in subdivision (a) may be made available only to one of the following:

(1) The person who is the subject of the record upon presentation of proper photo identification.

(2) A family member or legal representative of the person who is the subject of the record upon presentation of proper photo identification and certification of their relationship to the subject of the record.

(3) A county office that provides veteran's benefits services upon written request of that office.

(4) A United States official upon written request of that official. A public officer or employee is liable on his or her official bond for failure or refusal to render the services.

§ 6109. Every officer of a county or judicial district, upon receiving any fees for official duty or service, may be required by the person paying the fees to make out in writing and to deliver to the person a particular account of the fees. The account shall specify for what the fees, respectively, accrued, and the officer shall receipt it. If the officer refuses or neglects to do so when required, he is liable to the person paying the fees in treble the amount so paid.

§ 6110. Upon payment of the fees required by law, the officer shall perform the services required. For every failure or refusal to do so, the officer is liable upon his official bond.

§ 6203. (a) Every officer authorized by law to make or give any certificate or other writing is guilty of a misdemeanor if he or she makes and delivers as true any certificate or writing containing statements which he or she knows to be false.

(b) Notwithstanding any other limitation of time described in Section 802 of the Penal Code, or any other provision of law, prosecution for a violation of this offense shall be commenced within four years after discovery of the commission of the offense, or within four years after the completion of the offense, whichever is later.

(c) The penalty provided by this section is not an exclusive remedy, and does not affect any other relief or remedy provided by law.

§ 8200. The Secretary of State may appoint and commission notaries public in such number as the Secretary of State deems necessary for the public convenience. Notaries public may act as such notaries in any part of this state.

§ 8201. (a) Every person appointed as notary public shall meet all of the following requirements:

(1) Be at the time of appointment a legal resident of this state, except as otherwise provided in Section 8203.1.

(2) Be not less than 18 years of age.

(3) For appointments made on or after January 1, 2005, have satisfactorily completed a six-hour course of study approved by the Secretary of State pursuant to Section 8201.2 concerning the functions and duties of a notary public.

(4) Have satisfactorily completed a written examination prescribed by the Secretary of State to determine the fitness of the person to exercise the functions of the office of notary public. All questions shall be based on the law of this state as set forth in the booklet of the laws of California relating to notaries public distributed by the Secretary of State.

(b) (1) Commencing July 1, 2005, each applicant for notary public shall provide satisfactory proof that he or she has completed the course of study required pursuant to paragraph (3) of subdivision (a) prior to approval of his or her appointment by the Secretary of State.

(2) Commencing July 1, 2005, an applicant for notary public who holds a California notary public commission, and who has satisfactorily completed the six-hour course of study pursuant to paragraph (1) at least one time, shall provide satisfactory proof that he or she has satisfactorily completed a three-hour refresher course of study prior to reappointment as a notary public by the Secretary of State.

§ 8201.1. (a) Prior to granting an appointment as a notary public, the Secretary of State shall determine that the applicant possesses the required honesty, credibility, truthfulness, and integrity to fulfill the responsibilities of the position. To assist in determining the identity of the applicant and whether the applicant has been convicted of a disqualifying crime specified in subdivision (b) of Section 8214.1, the Secretary of State shall require that applicants be fingerprinted.

(b) Applicants shall submit to the Department of Justice fingerprint images and related information required by the department for the purpose of obtaining information as to the existence and content of a record of state and federal convictions and arrests and information as to the existence and content of a record of state and federal arrests for which the department establishes that the person is free on bail, or on his or her recognizance, pending trial or appeal.

(c) The department shall forward the fingerprint images and related information received pursuant to subdivision (a) to the Federal Bureau of Investigation and request a federal summary of criminal information.

(d) The department shall review the information returned from the Federal Bureau of Investigation and compile and disseminate a response to the Secretary of State pursuant to paragraph (1) of subdivision (p) of Section 11105 of the Penal Code.

(e) The Secretary of State shall request from the department subsequent arrest notification service, pursuant to Section 11105.2 of the Penal Code, for each person who submitted information pursuant to subdivision (a).

(f) The department shall charge a fee sufficient to cover the cost of processing the requests described in this section.

§ 8201.2. (a) The Secretary of State shall review the course of study proposed by any vendor to be offered pursuant to paragraph (3) of subdivision (a) and paragraph (2) of subdivision (b) of Section 8201. If the course of study includes all material that a person is expected to know to satisfactorily complete the written examination required pursuant to paragraph (4) of subdivision (a) of Section 8201, the Secretary of State shall approve the course of study.

(b) (1) The Secretary of State shall, by regulation, prescribe an application form and adopt a certificate of approval for the notary public education course of study proposed by a vendor.

(2) The Secretary of State may also provide a notary public education course of study.

(c) The Secretary of State shall compile a list of all persons offering an approved course of study pursuant to subdivision (a) and shall provide the list with every booklet of the laws of California relating to notaries public distributed by the Secretary of State.

(d) (1) A person who provides notary public education and violates any of the regulations adopted by the Secretary of State for approved vendors is subject to a civil penalty not to exceed one thousand dollars ($1,000) for each violation and shall be required to pay restitution where appropriate.

(2) The local district attorney, city attorney, or the Attorney General may bring a civil action to recover the civil penalty prescribed pursuant to this subdivision. A public prosecutor shall inform the Secretary of State of any civil penalty imposed under this section.

§ 8201.5. The Secretary of State shall require an applicant for appointment and commission as a notary public to complete an application form and submit a photograph of their person as prescribed by the Secretary of State. Information on this form filed by an applicant with the Secretary of State, except for his or her name and address, is confidential and no individual record shall be divulged by an official or employee having access to it to any person other than the applicant, his or her authorized representative, or an employee or officer of the federal government, the state government, or a local agency, as defined in subdivision (b) of Section 6252 of the Government Code, acting in his or her official capacity. That information shall be used by the Secretary of State for the sole purpose of carrying out the duties of this chapter.

§ 8202. (a) When executing a jurat, a notary shall administer an oath or affirmation to the affiant and shall determine, from satisfactory evidence as described in Section 1185 of the Civil Code, that the affiant is the person executing the document. The affiant shall sign the document in the presence of the notary.

(b) To any affidavit subscribed and sworn to before a notary, there shall be attached a jurat in the following form:

State of California
County of _____

Subscribed and sworn to (or affirmed) before me on this _____ day of
_____, 20__, by _____, proved to me on the basis of
satisfactory evidence to be the person(s) who appeared before me.

Seal_____
Signature_____

§ 8202.5. The Secretary of State may appoint and commission the number
of state, city, county, and public school district employees as notaries public
to act for and on behalf of the governmental entity for which appointed which
the Secretary of State deems proper. Whenever a notary is appointed and
commissioned, a duly authorized representative of the employing governmental
entity shall execute a certificate that the appointment is made for the purposes
of the employing governmental entity, and whenever the certificate is filed with
any state or county officer, no fees shall be charged by the officer for the filing
or issuance of any document in connection with the appointment. The state
or any city, county, or school district for which the notary public is appointed
and commissioned pursuant to this section may pay from any funds available
for its support the premiums on any bond and the cost of any stamps, seals, or
other supplies required in connection with the appointment, commission, or
performance of the duties of the notary public.

Any fees collected or obtained by any notary public whose documents have
been filed without charge and for whom bond premiums have been paid by
the employer of the notary public shall be remitted by the notary public to the
employing agency which shall deposit the funds to the credit of the fund from
which the salary of the notary public is paid.

§ 8202.7. A private employer, pursuant to an agreement with an employee
who is a notary public, may pay the premiums on any bond and the cost of any
stamps, seals, or other supplies required in connection with the appointment,
commission, or performance of the duties of such notary public. Such agreement
may also provide for the remission of fees collected by such notary public to the
employer, in which case any fees collected or obtained by such notary public
while such agreement is in effect shall be remitted by such notary public to the
employer which shall deposit such funds to the credit of the fund from which the
compensation of the notary public is paid.

§ 8202.8. Notwithstanding any other provision of law, a private employer
of a notary public who has entered into an agreement with his or her employee
pursuant to Section 8202.7 may limit, during the employee's ordinary course
of employment, the providing of notarial services by the employee solely to
transactions directly associated with the business purposes of the employer.

§ 8203.1. The Secretary of State may appoint and commission notaries public
for the military and naval reservations of the Army, Navy, Coast Guard, Air Force,
and Marine Corps of the United States, wherever located in the state; provided,
however, that the appointee shall be a citizen of the United States, not less than
18 years of age, and must meet the requirements set forth in paragraphs (3) and
(4) of subdivision (a) of Section 8201.

§ 8203.2. Such notaries public shall be appointed only upon the
recommendation of the commanding officer of the reservation in which they
are to act, and they shall be authorized to act only within the boundaries of this
reservation.

§ 8203.3. In addition to the qualifications established in Section 8203.1, appointment will be made only from among those persons who are federal civil service employees at the reservation in which they will act as notaries public.

§ 8203.4. The term of office shall be as set forth in Section 8204, except that the appointment shall terminate if the person shall cease to be employed as a federal civil service employee at the reservation for which appointed. The commanding officer of the reservation shall notify the Secretary of State of termination of employment at the reservation for which appointed within 30 days of such termination. A notary public whose appointment terminates pursuant to this section will have such termination treated as a resignation.

§ 8203.5. In addition to the name of the State, the jurat shall also contain the name of the reservation in which the instrument is executed.

§ 8203.6. No fees shall be collected by such notaries public for service rendered within the reservation in the capacity of a notary public.

§ 8204. The term of office of a notary public is for four years commencing with the date specified in the commission.

§ 8204.1. The Secretary of State may cancel the commission of a notary public if a check or other remittance accepted as payment for the examination, application, commission, and fingerprint fee is not paid upon presentation to the financial institution upon which the check or other remittance was drawn. Upon receiving written notification that the item presented for payment has not been honored for payment, the Secretary of State shall first give a written notice of the applicability of this section to the notary public or the person submitting the instrument. Thereafter, if the amount is not paid by a cashier's check or the equivalent, the Secretary of State shall give a second written notice of cancellation and the cancellation shall thereupon be effective. This second notice shall be given at least 20 days after the first notice, and no more than 90 days after the commencement date of the commission.

§ 8205. (a) It is the duty of a notary public, when requested: (1) To demand acceptance and payment of foreign and inland bills of exchange, or promissory notes, to protest them for nonacceptance and nonpayment, and, with regard only to the nonacceptance or nonpayment of bills and notes, to exercise any other powers and duties that by the law of nations and according to commercial usages, or by the laws of any other state, government, or country, may be performed by notaries.

(2) To take the acknowledgment or proof of advance health care directives, powers of attorney, mortgages, deeds, grants, transfers, and other instruments of writing executed by any person, and to give a certificate of that proof or acknowledgment, endorsed on or attached to the instrument. The certificate shall be signed by the notary public in the notary public's own handwriting. A notary public may not accept any acknowledgment or proof of any instrument that is incomplete.

(3) To take depositions and affidavits, and administer oaths and affirmations, in all matters incident to the duties of the office, or to be used before any court, judge, officer, or board. Any deposition, affidavit, oath, or affirmation shall be signed by the notary public in the notary public's own handwriting.

(4) To certify copies of powers of attorney under Section 4307 of the Probate Code. The certification shall be signed by the notary public in the notary public's own handwriting.

(b) It shall further be the duty of a notary public, upon written request:

(1) To furnish to the Secretary of State certified copies of the notary's journal.

(2) To respond within 30 days of receiving written requests sent by certified mail from the Secretary of State's office for information relating to official acts performed by the notary.

§ 8206. (a) (1) A notary public shall keep one active sequential journal at a time, of all official acts performed as a notary public. The journal shall be kept in a locked and secured area, under the direct and exclusive control of the notary. Failure to secure the journal shall be cause for the Secretary of State to take administrative action against the commission held by the notary public pursuant to Section 8214.1.

(2) The journal shall be in addition to, and apart from, any copies of notarized documents that may be in the possession of the notary public and shall include all of the following:

(A) Date, time, and type of each official act.

(B) Character of every instrument sworn to, affirmed, acknowledged, or proved before the notary.

(C) The signature of each person whose signature is being notarized.

(D) A statement as to whether the identity of a person making an acknowledgment or taking an oath or affirmation was based on satisfactory evidence. If identity was established by satisfactory evidence pursuant to Section 1185 of the Civil Code, the journal shall contain the signature of the credible witness swearing or affirming to the identity of the individual or the type of identifying document, the governmental agency issuing the document, the serial or identifying number of the document, and the date of issue or expiration of the document.

(E) If the identity of the person making the acknowledgment or taking the oath or affirmation was established by the oaths or affirmations of two credible witnesses whose identities are proven to the notary public by presentation of any document satisfying the requirements of paragraph (3) or (4) of subdivision (b) of Section 1185 of the Civil Code, the notary public shall record in the journal the type of documents identifying the witnesses, the identifying numbers on the documents identifying the witnesses, and the dates of issuance or expiration of the documents presented identifying the witnesses.

(F) The fee charged for the notarial service.

(G) If the document to be notarized is a deed, quitclaim deed, deed of trust affecting real property, or a power of attorney document, the notary public shall require the party signing the document to place his or her right thumbprint in the journal. If the right thumbprint is not available, then the notary shall have the party use his or her left thumb, or any available finger and shall so indicate in the journal. If the party signing the document is physically unable to provide a thumbprint or fingerprint, the notary shall so indicate in the journal and shall also provide an explanation of that physical condition. This paragraph shall not apply to a trustee's deed resulting from a decree of foreclosure or a nonjudicial foreclosure pursuant to Section 2924 of the Civil Code, nor to a deed of reconveyance.

(b) If a sequential journal of official acts performed by a notary public is stolen, lost, misplaced, destroyed, damaged, or otherwise rendered unusable as a record of notarial acts and information, the notary public shall immediately notify the Secretary of State by certified or registered mail. The notification shall include the period of the journal entries, the notary public commission number, and the expiration date of the commission, and when applicable, a photocopy of any police report that specifies the theft of the sequential journal of official acts.

(c) Upon written request of any member of the public, which request shall include the name of the parties, the type of document, and the month and year in which notarized, the notary shall supply a photostatic copy of the line item representing the requested transaction at a cost of not more than thirty cents ($0.30) per page.

(d) The journal of notarial acts of a notary public is the exclusive property of that notary public, and shall not be surrendered to an employer upon termination of employment, whether or not the employer paid for the journal, or at any other time. The notary public shall not surrender the journal to any other person, except the county clerk, pursuant to Section 8209, or immediately, or if the journal is not present then as soon as possible, upon request to a peace officer investigating a criminal offense who has reasonable suspicion to believe the journal contains evidence of a criminal offense, as defined in Sections 830.1, 830.2, and 830.3 of the Penal Code, acting in his or her official capacity and within his or her authority. If the peace officer seizes the notary journal, he or she must have probable cause as required by the laws of this state and the United States. A peace officer or law enforcement agency that seizes a notary journal shall notify the Secretary of State by facsimile within 24 hours, or as soon possible thereafter, of the name of the notary public whose journal has been seized. The notary public shall obtain a receipt for the journal, and shall notify the Secretary of State by certified mail within 10 days that the journal was relinquished to a peace officer. The notification shall include the period of the journal entries, the commission number of the notary public, the expiration date of the commission, and a photocopy of the receipt. The notary public shall obtain a new sequential journal. If the journal relinquished to a peace officer is returned to the notary public and a new journal has been obtained, the notary public shall make no new entries in the returned journal. A notary public who is an employee shall permit inspection and copying of journal transactions by a duly designated auditor or agent of the notary public's employer, provided that the inspection and copying is done in the presence of the notary public and the transactions are directly associated with the business purposes of the employer. The notary public, upon the request of the employer, shall regularly provide copies of all transactions that are directly associated with the business purposes of the employer, but shall not be required to provide copies of any transaction that is unrelated to the employer's business. Confidentiality and safekeeping of any copies of the journal provided to the employer shall be the responsibility of that employer.

(e) The notary public shall provide the journal for examination and copying in the presence of the notary public upon receipt of a subpoena duces tecum or a court order, and shall certify those copies if requested.

(f) Any applicable requirements of, or exceptions to, state and federal law shall apply to a peace officer engaged in the search or seizure of a sequential journal.

§ 8206.5. Upon receiving a request for a copy of a transaction pursuant to subdivision (c) of Section 8206, the notary shall respond to the request within 15 business days after receipt of the request and either supply the photostatic copy requested or acknowledge that no such line item exists. In a disciplinary proceeding for noncompliance with subdivision (c) of Section 8206 or this section, a notary may defend his or her delayed action on the basis of unavoidable, exigent business or personal circumstances.

§ 8207. A notary public shall provide and keep an official seal, which shall clearly show, when embossed, stamped, impressed or affixed to a document, the name of the notary, the State Seal, the words "Notary Public," and the name of the county wherein the bond and oath of office are filed, and the date the notary public's commission expires. The seal of every notary public commissioned on or after January 1, 1992, shall contain the sequential identification number assigned to the notary and the sequential identification number assigned to the manufacturer or vendor. The notary public shall authenticate with the official seal all official acts. A notary public shall not use the official notarial seal except for the purpose of carrying out the duties and responsibilities as set forth in this chapter. A notary public shall not use the title "notary public" except for the purpose of rendering notarial service.

The seal of every notary public shall be affixed by a seal press or stamp that will print or emboss a seal which legibly reproduces under photographic methods the required elements of the seal. The seal may be circular not over two inches in diameter, or may be a rectangular form of not more than one inch in width by two and one-half inches in length, with a serrated or milled edged border, and shall contain the information required by this section. The seal shall be kept in a locked and secured area, under the direct and exclusive control of the notary. Failure to secure the seal shall be cause for the Secretary of State to take administrative action against the commission held by the notary public pursuant to Section 8214.1.

The official seal of a notary public is the exclusive property of that notary public, and shall not be surrendered to an employer upon the termination of employment, whether or not the employer paid for the seal, or to any other person. The notary, or his or her representative, shall destroy or deface the seal upon termination, resignation, or revocation of the notary's commission.

§ 8207.1. The Secretary of State shall assign a sequential identification number to each notary which shall appear on the notary commission.

§ 8207.2. (a) No notary seal or press stamp shall be manufactured, duplicated, sold, or offered for sale unless authorized by the Secretary of State.

(b) The Secretary of State shall develop and implement procedures and guidelines for the issuance of notary seals on or before January 1, 1992.

(c) The Secretary of State shall issue a permit with a sequential identification number to each manufacturer or vendor authorized to issue notary seals. The Secretary of State may establish a fee for the issuance of the permit which shall not exceed the actual costs of issuing the permit.

(d) The Secretary of State shall develop a certificate of authorization to purchase a notary stamp from an authorized vendor.

(e) The certificate of authorization shall be designed to prevent forgeries and shall contain a sequential identification number.

§ 8207.3. (a) The Secretary of State shall issue certificates of authorization with which a notary public can obtain an official notary seal.

(b) A vendor or manufacturer is authorized to provide a notary with an official seal only upon presentation by the notary public of a certificate of authorization.

(c) A vendor of official seals shall note the receipt of certificates of authorization and sequential identification numbers of certificates presented by a notary public upon a certificate of authorization.

(d) A copy of a certificate of authorization shall be retained by a vendor and the original, which shall contain a sample impression of the seal issued to the notary public, shall be submitted to the Secretary of State for verification and recordkeeping. The Secretary of State shall develop guidelines for submitting certificates of authorization by vendors.

(e) Any notary whose official seal is lost, misplaced, destroyed, broken, damaged, or is rendered otherwise unworkable shall immediately mail or deliver written notice of that fact to the Secretary of State. The Secretary of State, within five working days after receipt of the notice, if requested by a notary, shall issue a certificate of authorization which a notary may use to obtain a replacement seal.

§ 8207.4. (a) Any person who willfully violates any part of Section 8207.1, 8207.2, 8207.3, or 8207.4 shall be subject to a civil penalty not to exceed one thousand five hundred dollars ($1,500) for each violation, which may be recovered in a civil action brought by the Attorney General or the district attorney or city attorney, or by a city prosecutor in any city and county.

(b) The penalty provided by this section is not an exclusive remedy, and does not affect any other relief or remedy provided by law.

§ 8208. The protest of a notary public, under his or her hand and official seal, of a bill of exchange or promissory note for nonacceptance or nonpayment, specifying any of the following is prima facie evidence of the facts recited therein:

(a) The time and place of presentment.

(b) The fact that presentment was made and the manner thereof.

(c) The cause or reason for protesting the bill.

(d) The demand made and the answer given, if any, or the fact that the drawee or acceptor could not be found.

§ 8209. (a) If any notary public resigns, is disqualified, removed from office, or allows his or her appointment to expire without obtaining reappointment within 30 days, all notarial records and papers shall be delivered within 30 days to the clerk of the county in which the notary public's current official oath of office is on file. If the notary public willfully fails or refuses to deliver all notarial records and papers to the county clerk within 30 days, the person is guilty of a misdemeanor and shall be personally liable for damages to any person injured by that action or inaction.

(b) In the case of the death of a notary public, the personal representative of the deceased shall promptly notify the Secretary of State of the death of the notary public and shall deliver all notarial records and papers of the deceased to the clerk of the county in which the notary public's official oath of office is on file.

(c) After 10 years from the date of deposit with the county clerk, if no request for, or reference to such records has been made, they may be destroyed upon order of court.

§ 8211. Fees charged by a notary public for the following services shall not exceed the fees prescribed by this section.

(a) For taking an acknowledgment or proof of a deed, or other instrument, to include the seal and the writing of the certificate, the sum of ten dollars ($10) for each signature taken.

(b) For administering an oath or affirmation to one person and executing the jurat, including the seal, the sum of ten dollars ($10).

(c) For all services rendered in connection with the taking of any deposition, the sum of twenty dollars ($20), and in addition thereto, the sum of five dollars ($5) for administering the oath to the witness and the sum of five dollars ($5) for the certificate to the deposition.

(d) For every protest for the nonpayment of a promissory note or for the nonpayment or nonacceptance of a bill of exchange, draft, or check, the sum of ten dollars ($10).

(e) For serving every notice of nonpayment of a promissory note or of nonpayment or nonacceptance of a bill of exchange, order, draft, or check, the sum of five dollars ($5).

(f) For recording every protest, the sum of five dollars ($5).

(g) No fee may be charged to notarize signatures on absentee ballot identification envelopes or other voting materials.

(h) For certifying a copy of a power of attorney under Section 4307 of the Probate Code the sum of ten dollars ($10).

(i) In accordance with section 6107, no fee may be charged to a United States military veteran for notarization of an application or a claim for a pension allotment, allowance, compensation, insurance, or any other veteran's benefit.

§ 8212. Every person appointed a notary public shall execute an official bond in the sum of fifteen thousand dollars ($15,000). The bond shall be in the form of a bond executed by an admitted surety insurer and not a deposit in lieu of bond.

§ 8213. (a) No later than 30 days after the beginning of the term prescribed in the commission, every person appointed a notary public shall file an official bond and an oath of office in the office of the county clerk of the county within which the person maintains a principal place of business as shown in the application submitted to the Secretary of State, and the commission shall not take effect unless this is done within the 30-day period. A person appointed to be a notary public shall take and subscribe the oath of office either in the office of that county clerk or before another notary public in that county. If the oath of office is taken and subscribed before a notary public, the oath and bond may be filed with the county clerk by certified mail. Upon the filing of the oath and bond, the county clerk shall immediately transmit to the Secretary of State a certificate setting forth the fact of the filing and containing a copy of the official oath, personally signed by the notary public in the form set forth in the commission and shall immediately deliver the bond to the county recorder for recording. The county clerk shall retain the oath of office for one year following the expiration of the term of the commission for which the oath was taken, after which the oath may be destroyed or otherwise disposed of. The copy of the oath, personally signed by the notary public, on file with the Secretary of State may at any time be read in evidence with like effect as the original oath, without further proof.

(b) If a notary public transfers the principal place of business from one county to another, the notary public may file a new oath of office and bond, or a duplicate of the original bond with the county clerk to which the principal place of business was transferred. If the notary public elects to make a new filing, the notary public shall, within 30 days of the filing, obtain an official seal which shall include the name of the county to which the notary public has transferred. In a case where the notary public elects to make a new filing, the same filing and recording fees are applicable as in the case of the original filing and recording of the bond.

(c) If a notary public submits an application for a name change to the Secretary of State, the notary public shall, within 30 days from the date an amended commission is issued, file a new oath of office and an amendment to the bond with the county clerk in which the principal place of business is located. The amended commission with the name change shall not take effect unless the filing is completed within the 30-day period. The amended commission with the name change takes effect the date the oath and amendment to the bond is filed with the county clerk. If the principal place of business address was changed in the application for name change, either a new or duplicate of the original bond shall be filed with the county clerk with the amendment to the bond. The notary public shall, within 30 days of the filing, obtain an official seal that includes the name of the notary public and the name of the county to which the notary public has transferred, if applicable.

(d) The recording fee specified in Section 27361 of the Government Code shall be paid by the person appointed a notary public. The fee may be paid to the county clerk who shall transmit it to the county recorder.

(e) The county recorder shall record the bond and shall thereafter mail, unless specified to the contrary, it to the person named in the instrument and, if no person is named, to the party leaving it for recording.

§ 8213.5. A notary public shall notify the Secretary of State by certified mail within 30 days as to any change in the location or address of the principal place of business or residence. A notary public shall not use a commercial mail receiving agency or post office box as his or her principal place of business or residence, unless the notary public also provides the Secretary of State with a physical street address as the principal place of residence. Willful failure to notify the Secretary of State of a change of address shall be punishable as an infraction by a fine of not more than five hundred dollars ($500).

§ 8213.6. If a notary public changes his or her name, the notary public shall complete an application for name change form and file that application with the Secretary of State. Information on this form shall be subject to the confidentiality provisions described in Section 8201.5. Upon approval of the name change form, the Secretary of State shall issue a commission that reflects the new name of the notary public. The term of the commission and commission number shall remain the same. Willful failure to notify the Secretary of State of a name change shall be punishable as an infraction by a fine of not more than five hundred dollars ($500).

§ 8214. For the official misconduct or neglect of a notary public, the notary public and the sureties on the notary public's official bond are liable in a civil action to the persons injured thereby for all the damages sustained.

§ 8214.1. The Secretary of State may refuse to appoint any person as notary public or may revoke or suspend the commission of any notary public upon any of the following grounds:

(a) Substantial and material misstatement or omission in the application submitted to the Secretary of State to become a notary public.

(b) Conviction of a felony, a lesser offense involving moral turpitude, or a lesser offense of a nature incompatible with the duties of a notary public. A conviction after a plea of nolo contendere is deemed to be a conviction within the meaning of this subdivision.

(c) Revocation, suspension, restriction, or denial of a professional license, if the revocation, suspension, restriction, or denial was for misconduct based on dishonesty, or for any cause substantially relating to the duties or responsibilities of a notary public.

(d) Failure to discharge fully and faithfully any of the duties or responsibilities required of a notary public.

(e) When adjudicated liable for damages in any suit grounded in fraud, misrepresentation, or for a violation of the state regulatory laws, or in any suit based upon a failure to discharge fully and faithfully the duties as a notary public.

(f) The use of false or misleading advertising wherein the notary public has represented that the notary public has duties, rights, or privileges that he or she does not possess by law.

(g) The practice of law in violation of Section 6125 of the Business and Professions Code.

(h) Charging more than the fees prescribed by this chapter.

(i) Commission of any act involving dishonesty, fraud, or deceit with the intent to substantially benefit the notary public or another, or substantially injure another.

(j) Failure to complete the acknowledgment at the time the notary's signature and seal are affixed to the document.

(k) Failure to administer the oath or affirmation as required by paragraph (3) of subdivision (a) of Section 8205.

(l) Execution of any certificate as a notary public containing a statement known to the notary public to be false.

(m) Violation of Section 8223.

(n) Failure to submit any remittance payable upon demand by the Secretary of State under this chapter or failure to satisfy any court-ordered money judgment, including restitution.

(o) Failure to secure the sequential journal of official acts, pursuant to Section 8206, or the official seal, pursuant to Section 8207, or willful failure to report the theft or loss of the sequential journal, pursuant to subdivision (b) of Section 8206.

(p) Violation of Section 8219.5.

(q) Commission of an act in violation of Section 6203, 8214.2, 8225, or 8227.3 of the Government Code or of Section 115, 470, 487, or 530.5 of the Penal Code.

(r) Willful failure to provide access to the sequential journal of official acts upon request by a peace officer.

§ 8214.15. (a) In addition to any commissioning or disciplinary sanction, a violation of subdivision (f), (i), (l), (m), or (p) of Section 8214.1 is punishable by a civil penalty not to exceed one thousand five hundred dollars ($1,500).

(b) In addition to any commissioning or disciplinary sanction, a violation of subdivision (h), (j), or (k) of Section 8214.1, or a negligent violation of subdivision (d) of Section 8214.1 is punishable by a civil penalty not to exceed seven hundred fifty dollars ($750).

(c) The civil penalty may be imposed by the Secretary of State if a hearing is not requested pursuant to Section 8214.3. If a hearing is requested, the hearing officer shall make the determination.

(d) Any civil penalties collected pursuant to this section shall be transferred to the General Fund. It is the intent of the Legislature that to the extent General Fund moneys are raised by penalties collected pursuant to this section, that money shall be made available to the Secretary of State's office to defray its costs of investigating and pursuing commissioning and monetary remedies for violations of the notary public law.

§ 8214.2. (a) A notary public who knowingly and willfully with intent to defraud performs any notarial act in relation to a deed of trust on real property consisting of a single-family residence containing not more than four dwelling units, with knowledge that the deed of trust contains any false statements or is forged, in whole or in part, is guilty of a felony.

(b) The penalty provided by this section is not an exclusive remedy and does not affect any other relief or remedy provided by law.

§ 8214.21. A notary public who willfully fails to provide access to the sequential journal of notarial acts when requested by a peace officer shall be subject to a civil penalty not exceeding two thousand five hundred dollars ($2,500). An action to impose a civil penalty under this subdivision may be brought by the Secretary of State in an administrative proceeding or any public prosecutor in superior court, and shall be enforced as a civil judgment. A public prosecutor shall inform the secretary of any civil penalty imposed under this section.

§ 8214.23. (a) A notary public who fails to obtain a thumbprint, as required by Section 8206, from a party signing a document shall be subject to a civil penalty not exceeding two thousand five hundred dollars ($2,500). An action to impose a civil penalty under this subdivision may be brought by the Secretary of State in an administrative proceeding or any public prosecutor in superior court, and shall be enforced as a civil judgment. A public prosecutor shall inform the secretary of any civil penalty imposed under this section.

(b) Notwithstanding any other limitation of time described in Section 802 of the Penal Code, or any other provision of law, prosecution for a violation of this offense shall be commenced within four years after discovery of the commission of the offense, or within four years after the completion of the offense, whichever is later

§ 8214.3. Prior to a revocation or suspension pursuant to this chapter or after a denial of a commission, or prior to the imposition of a civil penalty, the person affected shall have a right to a hearing on the matter and the proceeding shall be conducted in accordance with Chapter 5 (commencing with Section 11500) of Part 1 of Division 3, except that a person shall not have a right to a hearing after a denial of an application for a notary public commission in either of the following cases:

(a) The Secretary of State has, within one year previous to the application, and after proceedings conducted in accordance with Chapter 5 (commencing with Section 11500) of Part 1 of Division 3, denied or revoked the applicant's application or commission.

(b) The Secretary of State has entered an order pursuant to Section 8214.4 finding that the applicant has committed or omitted acts constituting grounds for suspension or revocation of a notary public's commission.

§ 8214.4. Notwithstanding this chapter or Chapter 5 (commencing with Section 11500) of Part 1 of Division 3, if the Secretary of State determines, after proceedings conducted in accordance with Chapter 5 (commencing with Section 11500) of Part 1 of Division 3, that any notary public has committed or omitted acts constituting grounds for suspension or revocation of a notary public's commission, the resignation or expiration of the notary public's commission shall not bar the Secretary of State from instituting or continuing an investigation or instituting disciplinary proceedings. Upon completion of the disciplinary proceedings, the Secretary of State shall enter an order finding the facts and stating the conclusion that the facts would or would not have constituted grounds for suspension or revocation of the commission if the commission had still been in effect.

§ 8214.5. Whenever the Secretary of State revokes the commission of any notary public, the Secretary of State shall file with the county clerk of the county in which the notary public's principal place of business is located a copy of the revocation. The county clerk shall note such revocation and its date upon the original record of such certificate.

§ 8214.8. Upon conviction of any offense in this chapter, or of section 6203, or of any felony, of a person commissioned as a notary public, in addition to any other penalty, the court shall revoke the commission of the notary public and shall require the notary public to surrender to the court the seal of the notary public. The court shall forward the seal, together with a certified copy of the judgment of conviction, to the Secretary of State.

§ 8216. When a surety of a notary desires to be released from responsibility on account of future acts, the release shall be pursuant to Article 11 (commencing with Section 996.110), and not by cancellation or withdrawal pursuant to Article 13 (commencing with Section 996.310), of Chapter 2 of Title 14 of Part 2 of the Code of Civil Procedure. For this purpose the surety shall make application to the superior court of the county in which the notary public's principal place of business is located and the copy of the application and notice of hearing shall be served on the Secretary of State as the beneficiary.

§ 8219.5. (a) Every notary public who is not an attorney who advertises the services of a notary public in a language other than English by signs or other means of written communication, with the exception of a single desk plaque, shall post with that advertisement a notice in English and in the other language which sets forth the following:

(1) This statement: I am not an attorney and, therefore, cannot give legal advice about immigration or any other legal matters.

(2) The fees set by statute which a notary public may charge.

(b) The notice required by subdivision (a) shall be printed and posted as prescribed by the Secretary of State.

(c) Literal translation of the phrase "notary public" into Spanish, hereby defined as "notario publico" or "notario," is prohibited.***

(d) The Secretary of State shall suspend for a period of not less than one year or revoke the commission of any notary public who fails to comply with subdivision (a) or (c). However, on the second offense the commission of such notary public shall be revoked permanently.

§ 8221. (a) If any person shall knowingly destroy, deface, or conceal any records or papers belonging to the office of a notary public, such person shall be guilty of a misdemeanor and be liable in a civil action for damages to any person injured as a result of such destruction, defacing, or concealment.

(b) Notwithstanding any other limitation of time described in Section 802 of the Penal Code, or any other provision of law, prosecution for a violation of this offense shall be commenced within four years after discovery of the commission of the offense, or within four years after the completion of the offense, whichever is later.

(c) The penalty provided by this section is not an exclusive remedy and does not affect any other relief or remedy provided by law.

§ 8222. (a) Whenever it appears to the Secretary of State that any person has engaged or is about to engage in any acts or practices which constitute or will constitute a violation of any provision of this chapter or any rule or regulation prescribed under the authority thereof, the Secretary of State may apply for an injunction, and upon a proper showing, any court of competent jurisdiction has power to issue a permanent or temporary injunction or restraining order to enforce the provisions of this chapter, and any party to the action has the right to prosecute an appeal from the order or judgment of the court.

(b) The court may order a person subject to an injunction or restraining order provided for in this section to reimburse the Secretary of State for expenses incurred in the investigation related to the petition. The Secretary of State shall refund any amount received as reimbursement should the injunction or restraining order be dissolved by an appellate court.

§ 8223. (a) No notary public who holds himself or herself out as being an immigration specialist, immigration consultant or any other title or description reflecting an expertise in immigration matters shall advertise in any manner whatsoever that he or she is a notary public.

(b) A notary public qualified and bonded as an immigration consultant under chapter 19.5 (commencing with Section 22440) of Division 8 of the Business and Professions Code may enter data, provided by the client, on immigration forms provided by a federal or state agency. The fee for this service shall not exceed ten dollars ($10) per individual for each set of forms. If notary services are performed in relation to the set of immigration forms, additional fees may be collected pursuant to Section 8211. This fee limitation shall not apply to an attorney, who is also a notary public, who is rendering professional services regarding immigration matters.

(c) Nothing in this section shall be construed to exempt a notary public who enters data on an immigration form at the direction of a client, or otherwise performs the services of an immigration consultant, as defined by Section 22441 of the Business and Professions Code, from the requirements of Chapter 19.5 (commencing with Section 22440) of Division 8 of the Business and Professions Code. A notary public who is not qualified and bonded as an immigration consultant under Chapter 19.5 (commencing with section 22440) of Division 8 of the Business and Professions Code may not enter data provided by a client on immigration forms nor otherwise perform the services of an immigration consultant.

§ 8224. A notary public who has a direct financial or beneficial interest in a transaction shall not perform any notarial act in connection with such transaction.

For purposes of this section, a notary public has a direct financial or beneficial interest in a transaction if the notary public:

(a) With respect to a financial transaction, is named, individually, as a principal to the transaction.

(b) With respect to real property, is named, individually, as a grantor, grantee, mortgagor, mortgagee, trustor, trustee, beneficiary, vendor, vendee, lessor, or lessee, to the transaction.

For purposes of this section, a notary public has no direct financial or beneficial interest in a transaction where the notary public acts in the capacity of an agent, employee, insurer, attorney, escrow, or lender for a person having a direct financial or beneficial interest in the transaction.

§ 8224.1. A notary public shall not take the acknowledgment or proof of instruments of writing executed by the notary public nor shall depositions or affidavits of the notary public be taken by the notary public.

§ 8225. (a) Any person who solicits, coerces, or in any manner influences a notary public to perform an improper notarial act knowing that act to be an improper notarial act, including any act required of a notary public under Section 8206, shall be guilty of a misdemeanor.

(b) Notwithstanding any other limitation of time described in Section 802 of the Penal Code, or any other provision of law, prosecution for a violation of this offense shall be commenced within four years after discovery of the commission of the offense, or within four years after the completion of the offense, whichever is later.

(c) The penalty provided by this section is not an exclusive remedy, and does not affect any other relief or remedy provided by law.

§ 8227.1. It shall be a misdemeanor for any person who is not a duly commissioned, qualified, and acting notary public for the State of California to do any of the following:

(a) Represent or hold himself or herself out to the public or to any person as being entitled to act as a notary public.

(b) Assume, use or advertise the title of notary public in such a manner as to convey the impression that the person is a notary public.

(c) Purport to act as a notary public.

§ 8227.3. Any person who is not a duly commissioned, qualified, and acting notary public who does any of the acts prohibited by Section 8227.1 in relation to any document or instrument affecting title to, placing an encumbrance on, or placing an interest secured by a mortgage or deed of trust on, real property consisting of a single-family residence containing not more than four dwelling units, is guilty of a felony.

§ 8228. The Secretary of State or a peace officer, as defined in Sections 830.1, 830.2, and 830.3 of the Penal Code, possessing reasonable suspicion and acting in his or her official capacity and within his or her authority, may enforce the provisions of this chapter through the examination of a notary public's books, records, letters, contracts, and other pertinent documents relating to the official acts of the notary public.

§ 8228.1. (a) Any notary public who willfully fails to perform any duty required of a notary public under Section 8206, or who willfully fails to keep the seal of the notary public under the direct and exclusive control of the notary public, or who surrenders the seal of the notary public to any person not otherwise authorized by law to possess the seal of the notary, shall be guilty of a misdemeanor.

(b) Notwithstanding any other limitation of time described in Section 802 of the Penal Code or any other provision of law, prosecution for a violation of this offense shall be commenced within four years after discovery of the commission of the offense, or within four years after the completion of the offense, whichever is later.

(c) The penalty provided by this section is not an exclusive remedy, and does not affect any other relief or remedy provided by law.

§ 8230. If a notary public executes a jurat and the statement sworn or subscribed to is contained in a document purporting to identify the affiant, and includes the birth date or age of the person and a purported photograph or finger or thumbprint of the person so swearing or subscribing, the notary public shall require, as a condition to executing the jurat, that the person verify the birth date or age contained in the statement by showing either:

(a) A certified copy of the person's birth certificate, or

(b) An identification card or driver's license issued by the Department of Motor Vehicles.

For the purposes of preparing for submission of forms required by the United States Immigration and Naturalization Service, and only for such purposes, a notary public may also accept for identification any documents or declarations acceptable to the United States Immigration and Naturalization Service.

§ 27201. (a) A notary acknowledgment shall be deemed complete for recording purposes without a photographically reproducible official seal of the notary public if the seal, as described in Section 8207, is present and legible, and the name of the notary, the county of the notary's principal place of business, the notary's telephone number, the notary's registration number, and the notary's commission expiration date are typed or printed in a manner that is photographically reproducible below, or immediately adjacent to, the notary's signature in the acknowledgment.

(b) If a request for a certified copy of a birth or death record is received by mail, a notarized statement sworn under penalty of perjury shall accompany the request, stating that the requester is an authorized person, as defined by law.

§ 27287. Unless it belongs to the class provided for in either Sections 27282 to 27286, inclusive, or Sections 1202 or 1203, of the Civil Code, or is a fictitious mortgage or deed of trust as provided in Sections 2952, or 2963, of the Civil Code, or is a fictitious oil and gas lease as provided in Section 1219 of the Civil Code, or is a claim of lien, as provided in Section 3084 of the Civil Code, or a notice of completion, as provided in Section 3093 of the Civil Code, before an instrument can be recorded its execution shall be acknowledged by the person executing it, or if executed by a corporation, by its president or secretary or other person executing it on behalf of the corporation, or, except for any quitclaim deed or grant deed other than a trustee's deed or a deed of reconveyance, mortgage, deed of trust, or security agreement, proved by subscribing witness or as provided in Sections 1198 and 1199 of the Civil Code, and the acknowledgment or proof certified as prescribed by law.

§ 27361. (a) The fee for recording and indexing every instrument, paper, or notice required or permitted by law to be recorded shall not exceed ten dollars ($10) for recording the first page and three dollars ($3) for each additional page, except the recorder may charge additional fees as follows:

(1) If the printing on printed forms is spaced more than nine lines per vertical inch or more than 22 characters and spaces per inch measured horizontally for not less than 3 inches in one sentence, the recorder shall charge one dollar ($1) extra for each page or sheet on which printing appears excepting, however, the extra charge shall not apply to printed words which are directive or explanatory in nature for completion of the form or on vital statistics forms. Fees collected under this paragraph are not subject to subdivision (b) or (c).

(2) If a page or sheet does not conform with the dimensions described in subdivision (a) of Section 27361.5, the recorder shall charge three dollars ($3) extra per page or sheet of the document. The extra charge authorized under this paragraph shall be available solely to support, maintain, improve, and provide for the full operation for modernized creation, retention, and retrieval of information in each county's system of recorded documents.***

§ 27361.5. (a) As used in Section 27361, a page shall be one printed side of a single piece of paper being 8½ inches by 11 inches.

(b) A sheet shall be one printed side of a single piece of paper which is not exactly 8½ inches by 11 inches but not greater than 8½ inches by 14 inches.

§ 27361.7. Whenever the text of a document presented for record may be made out but is not sufficiently legible to reproduce a readable photographic record, the recorder may require the person presenting it for record to substitute a legible original document or to prepare a legible copy of the first document by handwriting or typewriting and attach the same to the original as a part of the document for making the permanent photographic record. The handwritten or typewritten legible copy shall be certified by the party creating the copy under penalty of perjury as being a true copy of the original. As used in this section, the word "text" includes the notary seal, certificates, and other appendages thereto.

§ 27390. (a) This article shall be known and may be cited as the Electronic Recording Delivery Act of 2004. ***

(e) When a signature is required to be accompanied by a notary's seal or stamp, that requirement is satisfied if the electronic signature of the notary contains all of the following:

(1) The name of the notary.

(2) The words "Notary Public."

(3) The name of the county where the bond and oath of office of the notary are filed.

(4) The sequential identification number assigned to the notary, if any.

(5) The sequential identification number assigned to the manufacturer or vendor of the notary's physical or electronic seal, if any.

§ 66436. (a) A statement, signed and acknowledged by all parties having any record title interest in the subdivided real property, consenting to the preparation and recordation of the final map is required, ***

(c) A notary acknowledgment shall be deemed complete for recording without the official seal of the notary, so long as the name of the notary, the county of the notary's principal place of business, and the notary's commission expiration date are typed or printed below or immediately adjacent to the notary's signature in the acknowledgment.

Business and Professions Code

§ 6125. No person shall practice law in California unless the person is an active member of the State Bar.

§ 6126. (a) Any person advertising or holding himself or herself out as practicing or entitled to practice law or otherwise practicing law who is not an active member of the State Bar, is guilty of a misdemeanor. ***

§ 6127. The following acts or omissions in respect to the practice of law are contempts of the authority of the courts:

(a) Assuming to be an officer or attorney of a court and acting as such, without authority.

(b) Advertising or holding oneself out as practicing or as entitled to practice law or otherwise practicing law in any court, without being an active member of the State Bar.

Proceedings to adjudge a person in contempt of court under this section are to be taken in accordance with the provisions of Title V of Part III of the Code of Civil Procedure.

§ 22442.2. (a) An immigration consultant shall conspicuously display in his or her office a notice that shall be at least 12 inches by 20 inches with boldface type or print with each character at least one inch in height and width in English and in the native language of the consultant's clientele, the following information:

(1) The full name, address, and evidence of compliance with any applicable bonding requirement including the bond number, if any.

(2) A statement that the consultant is not an attorney.

(b) Prior to providing any services, an immigration consultant shall provide the client with written disclosure which shall include the immigration consultant's name, address, telephone number, agent for service of process, and evidence of compliance with any applicable bonding requirement, including the bond number, if any.

§ 22442.3. An immigration consultant shall not, with the intent to mislead, literally translate, from English into another language, the words or titles, including, but not limited to, "notary public," "notary," "licensed," "attorney," "lawyer," or any other terms that imply that the person is an attorney, in any document, including an advertisement, stationery, letterhead, business card, or other comparable written material describing the immigration consultant.

(b) For purposes of this section, "literal translation" of a word or phrase from one language means the translation of a word or phrase without regard to the true meaning of the word or phrase in the language that is being translated.

(c) An immigration consultant may not make or authorize the making of any verbal or written references to his or her compliance with the bonding requirements of Section 22443.1 except as provided in this chapter.

Civil Code

§ 14. Words used in this code in the present tense include the future as well as the present; words used in the masculine gender include the feminine and neuter; the singular number includes the plural, and the plural the singular; the word person includes a corporation as well as a natural person; county includes city and county; writing includes printing and typewriting; oath includes affirmation or declaration; and every mode of oral statement, under oath or affirmation, is embraced by the term "testify," and every written one in the term "depose"; signature or subscription includes mark, when the person cannot write, his name being written near it, by a person who writes his own name as a witness; provided, that when a signature is by mark it must in order that the same may be acknowledged or may serve as the signature to any sworn statement be witnessed by two persons who must subscribe their own names as witnesses thereto. *******

§ 1181. The proof or acknowledgment of an instrument may be made before a notary public at any place within this state, or within the county or city and county in this state in which the officer specified below was elected or appointed, before either:

(a) A clerk of a superior, municipal, or justice court.

(b) A county clerk.

(c) A court commissioner.

(d) A judge or retired judge of a municipal or justice court.

(e) A district attorney.

(f) A clerk of a board of supervisors.

(g) A city clerk.

(h) A county counsel.

(i) A city attorney.

(j) Secretary of the Senate.

(k) Chief Clerk of the Assembly.

§ 1182. The proof or acknowledgment of an instrument may be made without this state, but within the United States, and within the jurisdiction of the officer, before any of the following:

(1) A justice, judge, or clerk of any court of record of the United States.

(2) A justice, judge, or clerk of any court of record of any state.

(3) A commissioner appointed by the Governor or Secretary of State for that purpose.

(4) A notary public.

(5) Any other officer of the state where the acknowledgment is made authorized by its laws to take such proof or acknowledgment.

§ 1183. The proof or acknowledgment of an instrument may be made without the United States, before any of the following:

(a) A minister, commissioner, or charge d'affaires of the United States, resident and accredited in the country where the proof or acknowledgment is made.

(b) A consul, vice consul, or consular agent of the United States, resident in the country where the proof or acknowledgment is made.

(c) A judge of a court of record of the country where the proof or acknowledgment is made.

(d) Commissioners appointed by the Governor or Secretary of State for that purpose.

(e) A notary public.

If the proof or acknowledgment is made before a notary public, the signature of the notary public shall be proved or acknowledged (1) before a judge of a court of record of the country where the proof or acknowledgment is made, or (2) by any American diplomatic officer, consul general, consul, vice consul, or consular agent, or (3) by an apostille (certification) affixed to the instrument pursuant to the terms of The Hague Convention Abolishing the Requirement of Legalization for Foreign Public Documents.

§ 1183.5. Any officer on active duty or performing inactive-duty training in the armed forces having the general powers of a notary public pursuant to Section 936 or 1044a of Title 10 of the United States Code (Public Law 90-632 and 101-510) and any successor statutes may perform all notarial acts for any person serving in the armed forces of the United States, wherever he or she may be, or for any spouse of a person serving in the armed forces, wherever he or she may be, or for any person eligible for legal assistance under laws and regulations of the United States, wherever he or she may be, for any person serving with, employed by, or accompanying such armed forces outside the United States and outside the Canal Zone, Puerto Rico, Guam and the Virgin Islands, and any person subject to the Uniform Code of Military Justice outside of the United States.

Any instrument acknowledged by any such officer or any oath or affirmation made before such officer shall not be rendered invalid by the failure to state therein the place of execution or acknowledgment. No seal or authentication of the officer's certificate of acknowledgment or of any jurat signed by him or her shall be required but the officer taking the acknowledgment shall endorse thereon or attach thereto a certificate substantially in a form authorized by the laws of this state or in the following form:

On this the _____ day of _____, 20__, before me _____, the undersigned officer, personally appeared _____ known to me (or satisfactorily proven) to be (a) serving in the armed forces of the United States, (b) a spouse of a person serving in the armed forces of the United States, or (c) a person serving with, employed by, or accompanying the armed forces of the United States outside the United States and outside the Canal Zone, Puerto Rico, Guam, and the Virgin Islands, and to be the person whose name is subscribed to the within instrument and acknowledged that he or she executed the same. And the undersigned does further certify that he or she is at the date of this certificate a commissioned officer of the armed forces of the United States having the general powers of a notary public under the provisions of Section 936 or 1044a of Title 10 of the United States Code (Public Law 90-632 and 101-510).

_____ Signature of officer,
_____ rank, branch of service and capacity in which signed.

To any affidavit subscribed and sworn to before such officer there shall be attached a jurat substantially in the following form:

Subscribed and sworn to before me on this ____ day of _____, 19__.
_____ Signature of officer, _____ rank, branch of service and capacity in which signed.

The recitals contained in any such certificate or jurat shall be prima facie evidence of the truth thereof, and any certificate of acknowledgment, oath or affirmation purporting to have been made by any commissioned officer of the Army, Air Force, Navy, Marine Corps or Coast Guard shall, notwithstanding the omission of any specific recitals therein, constitute presumptive evidence of the existence of the facts necessary to authorize such acknowledgment, oath or affirmation to be taken by the certifying officer pursuant to this section.

§ 1185. (a) The acknowledgment of an instrument shall not be taken unless the officer taking it has satisfactory evidence that the person making the acknowledgment is the individual who is described in and who executed the instrument.

(b) For the purposes of this section "satisfactory evidence" means the absence of any information, evidence, or other circumstances that would lead a reasonable person to believe that the person making the acknowledgment is not the individual he or she claims to be and any one of the following:

(1) (A) The oath or affirmation of a credible witness personally known to the officer, whose identity is proven to the officer upon presentation of any document satisfying the requirements of paragraph (3) or (4), that the person making the acknowledgment is personally known to the witness and that each of the following are true:

(i) The person making the acknowledgment is the person named in the document.

(ii) The person making the acknowledgment is personally known to the witness.

(iii) That it is the reasonable belief of the witness that the circumstances of the person making the acknowledgment are such that it would be very difficult or impossible for that person to obtain another form of identification.

(iv) The person making the acknowledgment does not possess any of the identification documents named in paragraphs (3) and (4).

(v) The witness does not have a financial interest in the document being acknowledged and is not named in the document.

(B) A notary public who violates this section by failing to obtain the satisfactory evidence required by subparagraph (A) shall be subject to a civil penalty not exceeding ten thousand dollars ($10,000). An action to impose this civil penalty may be brought by the Secretary of State in an administrative proceeding or any public prosecutor in superior court, and shall be enforced as a civil judgment. A public prosecutor shall inform the secretary of any civil penalty imposed under this subparagraph.

(2) The oath or affirmation under penalty of perjury of two credible witnesses, whose identities are proven to the officer upon the presentation of any document satisfying the requirements of paragraph (3) or (4), that each statement in paragraph (1) of this subdivision is true.

(3) Reasonable reliance on the presentation to the officer of any one of the following, if the document is current or has been issued within five years:

(A) An identification card or driver's license issued by the California Department of Motor Vehicles.

(B) A passport issued by the Department of State of the United States.

(4) Reasonable reliance on the presentation of any one of the following, provided that a document specified in subparagraphs (A) to (F), inclusive, shall either be current or have been issued within five years and shall contain a photograph and description of the person named on it, shall be signed by the person, shall bear a serial or other identifying number, and, in the event that the document is a passport, shall have been stamped by the United States Immigration and Naturalization Service:

(A) A passport issued by a foreign government.

(B) A driver's license issued by a state other than California or by a Canadian or Mexican public agency authorized to issue drivers' licenses.

(C) An identification card issued by a state other than California.

(D) An identification card issued by any branch of the Armed Forces of the United States.

(E) An inmate identification card issued on or after January 1, 1988, by the Department of Corrections and Rehabilitation, if the inmate is in custody.

(F) An employee identification card issued by an agency or office of the State of California, or by an agency or office of a city, county, or city and county in this state.

(G) An inmate identification card issued prior to January 1, 1988, by the Department of Corrections and Rehabilitation, if the inmate is in custody.

(c) An officer who has taken an acknowledgment pursuant to this section shall be presumed to have operated in accordance with the provisions of law.

(d) Any party who files an action for damages based on the failure of the officer to establish the proper identity of the person making the acknowledgment shall have the burden of proof in establishing the negligence or misconduct of the officer.

(e) Any person convicted of perjury under this section shall forfeit any financial interest in the document.

§ 1188. An officer taking the acknowledgment of an instrument shall endorse thereon or attach thereto a certificate substantially in the form prescribed in Section 1189.

§ 1189. (a) (1) Any certificate of acknowledgment taken within this state shall be in the following form:

State of California   )
County of _____   )

On _____ before me, (here insert name and title of the officer), personally appeared _____ , who proved to me on the basis of satisfactory evidence to be the person(s) whose name(s) is/are subscribed to the within instrument and acknowledged to me that he/she/they executed the same in his/her/their authorized capacity(ies), and that by his/her/their signature(s) on the instrument the person(s), or the entity upon behalf of which the person(s) acted, executed the instrument.

I certify under PENALTY OF PERJURY under the laws of the State of California that the foregoing paragraph is true and correct.

WITNESS my hand and official seal.
Signature _____ (Seal)

(2) A notary public who willfully states as true any material fact that he or she knows to be false shall be subject to a civil penalty not exceeding ten thousand dollars ($10,000). An action to impose a civil penalty under this subdivision may be brought by the Secretary of State in an administrative proceeding or any public prosecutor in superior court, and shall be enforced as a civil judgment. A public prosecutor shall inform the secretary of any civil penalty imposed under this section.

(b) Any certificate of acknowledgment taken in another place shall be sufficient in this state if it is taken in accordance with the laws of the place where the acknowledgment is made.

(c) On documents to be filed in another state or jurisdiction of the United States, a California notary public may complete any acknowledgment form as may be required in that other state or jurisdiction on a document, provided the form does not require the notary to determine or certify that the signer holds a particular representative capacity or to make other determinations and certifications not allowed by California law.

(d) An acknowledgment provided prior to January 1, 1993, and conforming to applicable provisions of former Sections 1189, 1190, 1190a, 1190.1, 1191, and 1192, as repealed by Chapter 335 of the Statutes of 1990, shall have the same force and effect as if those sections had not been repealed.

§ 1190. The certificate of acknowledgment of an instrument executed on behalf of an incorporated or unincorporated entity by a duly authorized person in the form specified in Section 1189 shall be prima facie evidence that the instrument is the duly authorized act of the entity named in the instrument and shall be conclusive evidence thereof in favor of any good faith purchaser, lessee, or encumbrancer. "Duly authorized person," with respect to a domestic or foreign corporation, includes the president, vice president, secretary, and assistant secretary of the corporation.

§ 1193. Officers taking and certifying acknowledgments or proof of instruments for record, must authenticate their certificates by affixing thereto their signatures, followed by the names of their offices; also, their seals of office, if by the laws of the State or country where the acknowledgment or proof is taken, or by authority of which they are acting, they are required to have official seals.

§ 1195. (a) Proof of the execution of an instrument, when not acknowledged, may be made by any of the following:

1. By the party executing it, or either of them.
2. By a subscribing witness.
3. By other witnesses, in cases mentioned in Section 1198.

(b) Proof of the execution of a grant deed, mortgage, deed of trust, quitclaim deed, or security agreement is not permitted pursuant to Section 27287 of the Government Code, though proof of the execution of a trustee's deed or deed of reconveyance is permitted.

(c) Any certificate for proof of execution taken within this state may be in the following form, although the use of other, substantially similar forms is not precluded:

State of California   )

) ss.

County of _____   )

On _____ (date), before me, the undersigned, a notary public for the state, personally appeared _____ (subscribing witness' name), personally known to me (or proved to me on the oath of _____ [credible witness' name], who is personally known to me) to be the person whose name is subscribed to the within instrument, as a witness thereto, who, being by me duly sworn, deposed and said that he/she was present and saw _____ (name[s] of principal[s]), the same person[s] described in and whose name[s] is/are subscribed to the within and annexed instrument in his/her/their authorized capacity(ies) as (a) party(ies) thereto, execute the same, and that said affiant subscribed his/her name to the within instrument as a witness at the request of _____ (name[s] of principal[s]).

WITNESS my hand and official seal.

Signature _____ (seal)

§ 1196. A witness shall be proved to be a subscribing witness by the oath of a credible witness who provides the officer with any document satisfying the requirements of paragraph (3) or (4) of subdivision (b) of Section 1185.

§ 1197. The subscribing witness must prove that the person whose name is subscribed to the instrument as a party is the person described in it, and that such person executed it, and that the witness subscribed his name thereto as a witness.

§ 1363.03. a) An association shall adopt rules, in accordance with the procedures prescribed by Article 4 (commencing with Section 1357.100) of Chapter 2, that do all of the following:

(1) Ensure that if any candidate or member advocating a point of view is provided access to association media, newsletters, or Internet Web sites during a campaign, for purposes that are reasonably related to that election, equal access shall be provided to all candidates and members advocating a point of view, including those not endorsed by the board, for purposes that are reasonably related to the election. The association shall not edit or redact any content from these communications, but may include a statement specifying that the candidate or member, and not the association, is responsible for that content.

(2) Ensure access to the common area meeting space, if any exists, during a campaign, at no cost, to all candidates, including those who are not incumbents, and to all members advocating a point of view, including those not endorsed by the board, for purposes reasonably related to the election.

(3) Specify the qualifications for candidates for the board of directors and any other elected position, and procedures for the nomination of candidates. A nomination or election procedure shall not be deemed reasonable if it disallows any member of the association from nominating himself or herself for election to the board of directors.

(4) Specify the qualifications for voting, the voting power of each membership, the authenticity, validity, and effect of proxies, and the voting period for elections, including the times at which polls will open and close.

(5) Specify a method of selecting one or three independent third parties as inspector, or inspectors, of election utilizing one of the following methods:

(A) Appointment of the inspector or inspectors by the board.

(B) Election of the inspector or inspectors by the members of the association.

(C) Any other method for selecting the inspector or inspectors.

(b) Notwithstanding any other law or provision of the governing documents, an election within a common interest development regarding assessments, selection of members of the association board of directors, amendments to the governing documents, or the grant of exclusive use of common area property pursuant to Section 1363.07 shall be held by secret ballot in accordance with the procedures set forth in this section.

(c) (1) The association shall select an independent third party or parties as an inspector of election. The number of inspectors of election shall be one or three.

(2) For the purposes of this section, an independent third party includes, but is not limited to, a volunteer poll worker with the county registrar of voters, a licensee of the California Board of Accountancy, or a notary public. An independent third party may be a member of the association, but may not be a member of the board of directors or a candidate for the board of directors or related to a member of the board of directors or a candidate for the board of directors. An independent third party may not be a person who is currently employed or under contract to the association for any compensable services unless expressly authorized by rules of the association adopted pursuant to paragraph (5) of subdivision (a).

(3) The inspector or inspectors of election shall do all of the following:

(A) Determine the number of memberships entitled to vote and the voting power of each.

(B) Determine the authenticity, validity, and effect of proxies, if any.

(C) Receive ballots.

(D) Hear and determine all challenges and questions in any way arising out of or in connection with the right to vote.

(E) Count and tabulate all votes.

(F) Determine when the polls shall close.

(G) Determine the result of the election.

(H) Perform any acts as may be proper to conduct the election with fairness to all members in accordance with this section and all applicable rules of the association regarding the conduct of the election that are not in conflict with this section.

(4) An inspector of election shall perform his or her duties impartially, in good faith, to the best of his or her ability, and as expeditiously as is practical. If there are three inspectors of election, the decision or act of a majority shall be effective in all respects as the decision or act of all. Any report made by the inspector or inspectors of election is prima facie evidence of the facts stated in the report.

(d) Any instruction given in a proxy issued for an election that directs the manner in which the proxy holder is to cast the vote shall be set forth on a separate page of the proxy that can be detached and given to the proxy holder to retain. The proxy holder shall cast the member's vote by secret ballot.

(e) Ballots and two preaddressed envelopes with instructions on how to return ballots shall be mailed by first-class mail or delivered by the association to every member not less than 30 days prior to the deadline for voting. In order to preserve confidentiality, a voter may not be identified by name, address, or lot, parcel, or unit number on the ballot. The association shall use as a model those procedures used by California counties for ensuring confidentiality of voter absentee ballots, including all of the following:

(1) The ballot itself is not signed by the voter, but is inserted into an envelope that is sealed. This envelope is inserted into a second envelope that is sealed. In the upper left hand corner of the second envelope, the voter prints and signs his or her name, address, and lot, or parcel, or unit number that entitles him or her to vote.

(2) The second envelope is addressed to the inspector or inspectors of election, who will be tallying the votes. The envelope may be mailed or delivered by hand to a location specified by the inspector or inspectors of election. The member may request a receipt for delivery.

(f) All votes shall be counted and tabulated by the inspector or inspectors of election in public at a properly noticed open meeting of the board of directors or members. Any candidate or other member of the association may witness the counting and tabulation of the votes. No person, including a member of the association or an employee of the management company, shall open or otherwise review any ballot prior to the time and place at which the ballots are counted and tabulated.

(g) The results of the election shall be promptly reported to the board of directors of the association and shall be recorded in the minutes of the next meeting of the board of directors and shall be available for review by members of the association. Within 15 days of the election, the board shall publicize the results of the election in a communication directed to all members.

(h) The sealed ballots at all times shall be in the custody of the inspector or inspectors of election or at a location designated by the inspector or inspectors until after the tabulation of the vote, at which time custody shall be transferred to the association.

(i) After tabulation, election ballots shall be stored by the association in a secure place for no less than one year after the date of the election. In the event of a recount or other challenge to the election process, the association shall, upon written request, make the ballots available for inspection and review by association members or their authorized representatives. Any recount shall be conducted in a manner that shall preserve the confidentiality of the vote.

(j) The provisions of this section apply to both incorporated and unincorporated associations, notwithstanding any contrary provision of the governing documents.

§ 1633.1. This title may be cited as the Uniform Electronic Transaction Act.***

§ 1633.11. (a) If a law requires that a signature be notarized, the requirement is satisfied with respect to an electronic signature if an electronic record includes, in addition to the electronic signature to be notarized, the electronic signature of a notary public together with all other information required to be included in a notarization by other applicable law.

(b) In a transaction, if a law requires that a statement be signed under penalty of perjury, the requirement is satisfied with respect to an electronic signature, if an electronic record includes, in addition to the electronic signature, all of the information as to which the declaration pertains together with a declaration under penalty of perjury by the person who submits the electronic signature that the information is true and correct.

§ 1633.12. (a) If the law requires that a record be retained, the requirement is satisfied by retaining an electronic record of the information in the record, if the electronic record reflects accurately the information set forth in the record at the time it was first generated in its final form as an electronic record or otherwise, and the electronic record remains accessible for later reference. ***

Code of Civil Procedure

§ 335. The periods prescribed for the commencement of actions other than for the recovery of real property, are as follows:

§ 338. Within three years: ***

(f) (1) An action against a notary public on his or her bond or in his or her official capacity except that any cause of action based on malfeasance or misfeasance is not deemed to have accrued until discovery, by the aggrieved party or his or her agent, of the facts constituting the cause of action.

(2) Notwithstanding paragraph (1), an action based on malfeasance or misfeasance shall be commenced within one year from discovery, by the aggrieved party or his or her agent, of the facts constituting the cause of action or within three years from the performance of the notarial act giving rise to the action, whichever is later.

(3) Notwithstanding paragraph (1), an action against a notary public on his or her bond or in his or her official capacity shall be commenced within six years. ***

§ 1935. A subscribing witness is one who sees a writing executed or hears it acknowledged, and at the request of the party thereupon signs his name as a witness.

§ 2025. ***

(k) Except as provided in paragraph (3) of subdivision (d) of Section 2020, the deposition shall be conducted under the supervision of an officer who is authorized to administer an oath. This officer shall not be financially interested in the action and shall not be a relative or employee of any attorney of any of the parties, or of any of the parties. Any objection to the qualifications of the deposition officer is waived unless made before the deposition begins or as soon thereafter as the ground for that objection becomes known or could be discovered by reasonable diligence.

(l) (1) The deposition officer shall put the deponent under oath. Unless the parties agree or the court orders otherwise, the testimony, as well as any stated objections, shall be taken stenographically. The party noticing the deposition may also record the testimony by audiotape or videotape if the notice of deposition stated an intention also to record the testimony by either of those methods, or if all the parties agree that the testimony may also be recorded by either of those methods. Any other party, at that party's expense, may make a simultaneous audiotape or videotape record of the deposition, provided that other party promptly, and in no event less than three calendar days before the date for which the deposition is scheduled, serves a written notice of this intention to audiotape or videotape the deposition testimony on the party or attorney who noticed the deposition, on all other parties or attorneys on whom the deposition notice was served under subdivision (c), and on any deponent whose attendance is being compelled by a deposition subpoena under Section 2020. If this notice is given three calendar days before the deposition date, it shall be made by personal service under Section 1011. Examination and cross-examination of the deponent shall proceed as permitted at trial under the provisions of the Evidence Code. ***

§ 2026. ***

(c) A deposition taken under this section shall be conducted (1) under the supervision of a person who is authorized to administer oaths by the laws of the United States or those of the place where the examination is to be held, and who is not otherwise disqualified under subdivision (k) of Section 2025, or (2) before a person appointed by the court. This appointment is effective to authorize that person to administer oaths and to take testimony. When necessary or convenient, the court shall issue a commission on such terms and with such directions as are just and appropriate. ***

§ 2027. ***

(c) A deposition taken under this section shall be conducted (1) under the supervision of a person who is authorized to administer oaths or their equivalent by the laws of the United States or of the foreign nation, and who is not otherwise disqualified under subdivision (k) of Section 2025, or (2) a person or officer appointed by commission or under letters rogatory; or (3) any person agreed to by all the parties. ***

§ 2093. (a) Every court, every judge, or clerk of any court, every justice, and every notary public, and every officer or person authorized to take testimony in any action or proceeding, or to decide upon evidence, has the power to administer oaths or affirmations.

(b) Every shorthand reporter certified pursuant to Article 3 (commencing with Section 8020) of Chapter 13 of Division 3 of the Business and Professions Code has the power to administer oaths or affirmations and may perform the duties of the deposition officer pursuant to Section 2025. The certified shorthand reporter shall be entitled to receive fees for services rendered during a deposition, including fees for deposition services, as specified in subdivision (c) of Section 8211 of the Government Code.

(c) A former judge or justice of a court of record in this state who retired or resigned from office, other than a judge or justice who was retired by the Supreme Court for disability, shall have the power to administer oaths or affirmations, if the former judge or justice requests and receives a certification from the Commission on Judicial Performance that there was no formal disciplinary proceeding pending at the time of retirement or resignation. Where no formal disciplinary proceeding was pending at the time of retirement or resignation, the Commission on Judicial Performance shall issue the certification.

No law, rule, or regulation regarding the confidentiality of proceedings of the Commission on Judicial Performance shall be construed to prohibit the Commission on Judicial Performance from issuing a certificate as provided for in this section.

§ 2094. An oath, or affirmation, in an action or proceeding, may be administered as follows, the person who swears, or affirms, expressing his assent when addressed in the following form: "You do solemnly swear (or affirm, as the case may be), that the evidence you shall give in this issue (or matter), pending between ____ and ____, shall be the truth, the whole truth, and nothing but the truth, so help you God."

Elections Code

§ 8080. No fee or charge shall be made or collected by any officer for verifying any nomination document or circulator's affidavit.

Family Code

§ 503. The county clerk shall issue a confidential marriage license upon the request of a notary public approved by the county clerk to authorize confidential marriages pursuant to Chapter 2 (commencing with Section 530) and upon payment by the notary public of the fees specified in Sections 26840.1 and 26840.8 of the Government Code. The parties shall reimburse a notary public who authorizes a confidential marriage for the amount of the fees.

§ 530. (a) No notary public shall authorize a confidential marriage pursuant to this part unless the notary public is approved by the county clerk to authorize confidential marriages pursuant to this chapter.

(b) A violation of subdivision (a) is a misdemeanor punishable by a fine not to exceed one thousand dollars ($1,000) or six months in jail.

§ 531. (a) An application for approval to authorize confidential marriages pursuant to this part shall be submitted to the county clerk in the county in which the notary public who is applying for the approval resides. The county clerk shall exercise reasonable discretion as to whether to approve applications.

(b) The application shall include all of the following:

(1) The full name of the applicant.

(2) The date of birth of the applicant.

(3) The applicant's current residential address and telephone number.

(4) The address and telephone number of the place where the applicant will issue authorizations for the performance of a marriage.

(5) The full name of the applicant's employer if the applicant is employed by another person.

(6) Whether or not the applicant has engaged in any of the acts specified in Section 8214.1 of the Government Code.

(c) The application shall be accompanied by the fee provided for in Section 536.

§ 532. No approval shall be granted pursuant to this chapter unless the notary public shows evidence of successful completion of a course of instruction concerning the authorization of confidential marriages that shall be conducted by the county clerk. The course of instruction shall not exceed two hours.

§ 533. An approval to authorize confidential marriages pursuant to this chapter is valid for one year. The approval may be renewed for additional one-year periods upon payment of the renewal fee provided for in Section 536.

§ 534. (a) The county clerk shall maintain a list of the notaries public who are approved to authorize confidential marriages. The list shall be available for inspection by the public.

(b) It is the responsibility of a notary public approved to authorize confidential marriages pursuant to this chapter to keep current the information required in paragraphs (1), (3), (4), and (5) of subdivision (b) of Section 531. This information shall be used by the county clerk to update the list required to be maintained by this section.

§ 535. (a) If, after an approval to authorize confidential marriages is granted pursuant to this chapter, it is discovered that the notary public has engaged in any of the actions specified in Section 8214.1 of the Government Code, the approval shall be revoked, and any fees paid by the notary public may be retained by the county clerk.

(b) If a notary public who is approved to authorize confidential marriages pursuant to this chapter is alleged to have violated a provision of this division, the county clerk shall conduct a hearing to determine if the approval of the notary public should be suspended or revoked. The notary public may present such evidence as is necessary in the notary public's defense. If the county clerk determines that the notary public has violated a provision of this division, the county clerk may place the notary public on probation or suspend or revoke the notary public's registration, and any fees paid by the notary public may be retained by the county clerk. The county clerk shall report the findings of the hearing to the Secretary of State for whatever action the Secretary of State deems appropriate.

§ 536. (a) The fee for an application for approval to authorize confidential marriages pursuant to this chapter is three hundred dollars ($300).

(b) The fee for renewal of an approval is three hundred dollars ($300).

(c) Fees received pursuant to this chapter shall be deposited in a trust fund established by the county clerk. The money in the trust fund shall be used exclusively for the administration of the programs described in this chapter.

Penal Code

§ 17. (a) A felony is a crime which is punishable with death or by imprisonment in the state prison. Every other crime or public offense is a misdemeanor except those offenses that are classified as infractions. ***

§ 115.5. (a) Every person who files any false or forged document or instrument with the county recorder which affects title to, places an encumbrance on, or places an interest secured by a mortgage or deed of trust on, real property consisting of a single-family residence containing not more than four dwelling units, with knowledge that the document is false or forged, is punishable, in addition to any other punishment, by a fine not exceeding seventy-five thousand dollars ($75,000).

(b) Every person who makes a false sworn statement to a notary public, with knowledge that the statement is false, to induce the notary public to perform an improper notarial act on an instrument or document affecting title to, or placing an encumbrance on, real property consisting of a single-family residence containing not more than four dwelling units is guilty of a felony.

§ 118. (a) Every person who, having taken an oath that he or she will testify, declare, depose, or certify truly before any competent tribunal, officer, or person, in any of the cases in which the oath may by law of the State of California be administered, willfully and contrary to the oath, states as true any material matter which he or she knows to be false, and every person who testifies, declares, deposes, or certifies under penalty of perjury in any of the cases in which the testimony, declarations, depositions, or certification is permitted by law of the State of California under penalty of perjury and willfully states as true any material matter which he or she knows to be false, is guilty of perjury.

This subdivision is applicable whether the statement, or the testimony, declaration, deposition, or certification is made or subscribed within or without the State of California.

(b) No person shall be convicted of perjury where proof of falsity rests solely upon contradiction by testimony of a single person other than the defendant. Proof of falsity may be established by direct or indirect evidence.

§ 126. Perjury is punishable by imprisonment in the state prison for two, three or four years.

§ 470. ***

(b) Every person who, with the intent to defraud, counterfeits or forges the seal or handwriting of another is guilty of forgery.***

(d) Every person who, with the intent to defraud, falsely makes, alters, forges, or counterfeits, utters, publishes, passes or attempts or offers to pass, as true and genuine, any of the following items, knowing the same to be false, altered, forged, or counterfeited, is guilty of forgery: any check, bond, bank bill, or note, cashier's check, traveler's check, money order, post note, draft, any controller's warrant for the payment of money at the treasury, county order or warrant, or request for the payment of money, receipt for money or goods, bill of exchange, promissory note, order, or any assignment of any bond, writing obligatory, or other contract for money or other property, contract, due bill for payment of money or property, receipt for money or property, passage ticket, lottery ticket or share purporting to be issued under the California State Lottery Act of 1984, trading stamp, power of attorney, certificate of ownership or other document evidencing ownership of a vehicle or undocumented vessel, or any certificate of any share, right, or interest in the stock of any corporation or association, or the delivery of goods or chattels of any kind, or for the delivery of any instrument of writing, or acquittance, release or discharge of any debt, account, suit, action, demand, or any other thing, real or personal, or any transfer or assurance of money, certificate of shares of stock, goods, chattels, or other property whatever, or any letter of attorney, or other power to receive money, or to receive or transfer certificates of shares of stock or annuities, or to let, lease, dispose of, alien, or convey any goods, chattels, lands, or tenements, or other estate, real or personal, or falsifies the acknowledgment of any notary public, or any notary public who issues an acknowledgment knowing it to be false; or any matter described in subdivision (b).***

§ 472. Every person who, with intent to defraud another, forges, or counterfeits the seal of this State, the seal of any public officer authorized by law, the seal of any Court of record, or the seal of any corporation, or any other public seal authorized or recognized by the laws of this State, or of any other State, Government, or country, or who falsely makes, forges, or counterfeits any impression purporting to be an impression of any such seal, or who has in his possession any such counterfeited seal or impression thereof, knowing it to be counterfeited, and willfully conceals the same, is guilty of forgery.

§ 473. Forgery is punishable by imprisonment in the state prison, or by imprisonment in the county jail for not more than one year.

§ 653.55. It is a misdemeanor for any person for compensation to knowingly make a false or misleading material statement or assertion of fact in the preparation of an immigration matter which statement or assertion is detrimentally relied upon by another. Such a misdemeanor is punishable by imprisonment in the county jail not exceeding six months, or by a fine not exceeding two thousand five hundred dollars ($2,500), or by both.

§ 830. Any person who comes within the provisions of this chapter and who otherwise meets all standards imposed by law on a peace officer is a peace officer, and notwithstanding any other provision of law, no person other than those designated in this chapter is a peace officer. The restriction of peace officer functions of any public officer or employee shall not affect his or her status for purposes of retirement.

§ 830.1. (a) Any sheriff, undersheriff, or deputy sheriff, employed in that capacity, of a county, any chief of police of a city or chief, director, or chief executive officer of a consolidated municipal public safety agency that performs police functions, any police officer, employed in that capacity and appointed by the chief of police or chief, director, or chief executive of a public safety agency, of a city, any chief of police, or police officer of a district, including police officers of the San Diego Unified Port District Harbor Police, authorized by statute to maintain a police department, any marshal or deputy marshal of a superior court or county, any port warden or port police officer of the Harbor Department of the City of Los Angeles, or any inspector or investigator employed in that capacity in the office of a district attorney, is a peace officer. The authority of these peace officers extends to any place in the state, as follows:

(1) As to any public offense committed or which there is probable cause to believe has been committed within the political subdivision that employs the peace officer or in which the peace officer serves.

(2) Where the peace officer has the prior consent of the chief of police or chief, director, or chief executive officer of a consolidated municipal public safety agency, or person authorized by him or her to give consent, if the place is within a city or of the sheriff, or person authorized by him or her to give consent, if the place is within a county.

(3) As to any public offense committed or which there is probable cause to believe has been committed in the peace officer's presence, and with respect to which there is immediate danger to person or property, or of the escape of the perpetrator of the offense.

(b) The Attorney General and special agents and investigators of the Department of Justice are peace officers, and those assistant chiefs, deputy chiefs, chiefs, deputy directors, and division directors designated as peace officers by the Attorney General are peace officers. The authority of these peace officers extends to any place in the state where a public offense has been committed or where there is probable cause to believe one has been committed.

(c) Any deputy sheriff of the County of Los Angeles, and any deputy sheriff of the Counties of Butte, Glenn, Humboldt, Imperial, Inyo, Kern, Kings, Lassen, Mendocino, Plumas, Riverside, San Diego, Santa Barbara, Shasta, Siskiyou, Solano, Sonoma, Stanislaus, Sutter, Tehama, Tulare, and Tuolumne who is employed to perform duties exclusively or initially relating to custodial assignments with responsibilities for maintaining the operations of county custodial facilities, including the custody, care, supervision, security, movement, and transportation of inmates, is a peace officer whose authority extends to any place in the state only while engaged in the performance of the duties of his or her respective employment and for the purpose of carrying out the primary function of employment relating to his or her custodial assignments, or when performing other law enforcement duties directed by his or her employing agency during a local state of emergency.

§ 830.2. The following persons are peace officers whose authority extends to any place in the state:

(a) Any member of the Department of the California Highway Patrol including those members designated under subdivision (a) of Section 2250.1 of the Vehicle Code, provided that the primary duty of the peace officer is the enforcement of any law relating to the use or operation of vehicles upon the highways, or laws pertaining to the provision of police services for the protection of state officers, state properties, and the occupants of state properties, or both, as set forth in the Vehicle Code and Government Code.

(b) A member of the University of California Police Department appointed pursuant to Section 92600 of the Education Code, provided that the primary duty of the peace officer shall be the enforcement of the law within the area specified in Section 92600 of the Education Code.

(c) A member of the California State University Police Departments appointed pursuant to Section 89560 of the Education Code, provided that the primary duty of the peace officer shall be the enforcement of the law within the area specified in Section 89560 of the Education Code.

(d) (1) Any member of the Law Enforcement and Investigations Unit of the Department of Corrections, provided that the primary duties of the peace officer shall be the investigation or apprehension of parolees, parole violators, or escapees from state institutions, the transportation of those persons, and the coordination of those activities with other criminal justice agencies.

(2) Any member of the Office of Internal Affairs of the Department of Corrections, provided that the primary duties shall be criminal investigations of Department of Corrections personnel and the coordination of those activities with other criminal justice agencies. For purposes of this subdivision the member of the Office of Internal Affairs shall possess certification from the Commission on Peace Officer Standards and Training for investigators, or have completed training pursuant to Section 6126.1 of the Penal Code.

(e) Employees of the Department of Fish and Game designated by the director, provided that the primary duty of those peace officers shall be the enforcement of the law as set forth in Section 856 of the Fish and Game Code.

(f) Employees of the Department of Parks and Recreation designated by the director pursuant to Section 5008 of the Public Resources Code, provided that the primary duty of the peace officer shall be the enforcement of the law as set forth in Section 5008 of the Public Resources Code.

(g) The Director of Forestry and Fire Protection and employees or classes of employees of the Department of Forestry and Fire Protection designated by the director pursuant to Section 4156 of the Public Resources Code, provided that the primary duty of the peace officer shall be the enforcement of the law as that duty is set forth in Section 4156 of the Public Resources Code.

(h) Persons employed by the Department of Alcoholic Beverage Control for the enforcement of Division 9 (commencing with Section 23000) of the Business and Professions Code and designated by the Director of Alcoholic Beverage Control, provided that the primary duty of any of these peace officers shall be the enforcement of the laws relating to alcoholic beverages, as that duty is set forth in Section 25755 of the Business and Professions Code.

(i) Marshals and police appointed by the Board of Directors of the California Exposition and State Fair pursuant to Section 3332 of the Food and Agricultural Code, provided that the primary duty of the peace officers shall be the enforcement of the law as prescribed in that section.

(j) The Inspector General, pursuant to Section 6125, and the Chief Deputy Inspector General In Charge, the Senior Deputy Inspector General, the Deputy Inspector General, and those employees of the Inspector General as designated by the Inspector General, are peace officers, provided that the primary duty of these peace officers shall be conducting audits of investigatory practices and other audits, as well as conducting investigations, of the Department of Corrections, the Department of the Youth Authority, the Board of Prison Terms, the Youthful Offender Parole Board, or the Board of Corrections.

§ 830.3. The following persons are peace officers whose authority extends to any place in the state for the purpose of performing their primary duty or when making an arrest pursuant to Section 836 of the Penal Code as to any public offense with respect to which there is immediate danger to person or property, or of the escape of the perpetrator of that offense, or pursuant to Section 8597 or 8598 of the Government Code. These peace officers may carry firearms only if authorized and under those terms and conditions as specified by their employing agencies:

(a) Persons employed by the Division of Investigation of the Department of Consumer Affairs and investigators of the Medical Board of California and the Board of Dental Examiners, who are designated by the Director of Consumer Affairs, provided that the primary duty of these peace officers shall be the enforcement of the law as that duty is set forth in Section 160 of the Business and Professions Code.

(b) Voluntary fire wardens designated by the Director of Forestry and Fire Protection pursuant to Section 4156 of the Public Resources Code, provided that the primary duty of these peace officers shall be the enforcement of the law as that duty is set forth in Section 4156 of that code.

(c) Employees of the Department of Motor Vehicles designated in Section 1655 of the Vehicle Code, provided that the primary duty of these peace officers shall be the enforcement of the law as that duty is set forth in Section 1655 of that code.

(d) Investigators of the California Horse Racing Board designated by the board, provided that the primary duty of these peace officers shall be the enforcement of Chapter 4 (commencing with Section 19400) of Division 8 of the Business and Professions Code and Chapter 10 (commencing with Section 330) of Title 9 of Part 1 of this code.

(e) The State Fire Marshal and assistant or deputy state fire marshals appointed pursuant to Section 13103 of the Health and Safety Code, provided that the primary duty of these peace officers shall be the enforcement of the law as that duty is set forth in Section 13104 of that code.

(f) Inspectors of the food and drug section designated by the chief pursuant to subdivision (a) of Section 106500 of the Health and Safety Code, provided that the primary duty of these peace officers shall be the enforcement of the law as that duty is set forth in Section 106500 of that code.

(g) All investigators of the Division of Labor Standards Enforcement designated by the Labor Commissioner, provided that the primary duty of these peace officers shall be the enforcement of the law as prescribed in Section 95 of the Labor Code.

(h) All investigators of the State Departments of Health Services, Social Services, Mental Health, and Alcohol and Drug Programs, the Department of Toxic Substances Control, the Office of Statewide Health Planning and Development, and the Public Employees' Retirement System, provided that the primary duty of these peace officers shall be the enforcement of the law relating to the duties of his or her department or office. Notwithstanding any other provision of law, investigators of the Public Employees' Retirement System shall not carry firearms.

(i) The Chief of the Bureau of Fraudulent Claims of the Department of Insurance and those investigators designated by the chief, provided that the primary duty of those investigators shall be the enforcement of Section 550.

(j) Employees of the Department of Housing and Community Development designated under Section 18023 of the Health and Safety Code, provided that the primary duty of these peace officers shall be the enforcement of the law as that duty is set forth in Section 18023 of that code.

(k) Investigators of the office of the Controller, provided that the primary duty of these investigators shall be the enforcement of the law relating to the duties of that office. Notwithstanding any other law, except as authorized by the Controller, the peace officers designated pursuant to this subdivision shall not carry firearms.

(l) Investigators of the Department of Corporations designated by the Commissioner of Corporations, provided that the primary duty of these investigators shall be the enforcement of the provisions of law administered by the Department of Corporations. Notwithstanding any other provision of law, the peace officers designated pursuant to this subdivision shall not carry firearms.

(m) Persons employed by the Contractors' State License Board designated by the Director of Consumer Affairs pursuant to Section 7011.5 of the Business and Professions Code, provided that the primary duty of these persons shall be the enforcement of the law as that duty is set forth in Section 7011.5, and in Chapter 9 (commencing with Section 7000) of Division 3, of that code. The Director of Consumer Affairs may designate as peace officers not more than three persons who shall at the time of their designation be assigned to the special investigations unit of the board. Notwithstanding any other provision of law, the persons designated pursuant to this subdivision shall not carry firearms.

(n) The Chief and coordinators of the Law Enforcement Division of the Office of Emergency Services.

(o) Investigators of the office of the Secretary of State designated by the Secretary of State, provided that the primary duty of these peace officers shall be the enforcement of the law as prescribed in Chapter 3 (commencing with Section 8200) of Division 1 of Title 2 of, and Section 12172.5 of, the Government Code. Notwithstanding any other provision of law, the peace officers designated pursuant to this subdivision shall not carry firearms.

(p) The Deputy Director for Security designated by Section 8880.38 of the Government Code, and all lottery security personnel assigned to the California State Lottery and designated by the director, provided that the primary duty of any of those peace officers shall be the enforcement of the laws related to assuring the integrity, honesty, and fairness of the operation and administration of the California State Lottery.

(q) Investigators employed by the Investigation Division of the Employment Development Department designated by the director of the department, provided that the primary duty of those peace officers shall be the enforcement of the law as that duty is set forth in Section 317 of the Unemployment Insurance Code. Notwithstanding any other provision of law, the peace officers designated pursuant to this subdivision shall not carry firearms.

(r) The chief and assistant chief of museum security and safety of the California Science Center, as designated by the executive director pursuant to Section 4108 of the Food and Agricultural Code, provided that the primary duty of those peace officers shall be the enforcement of the law as that duty is set forth in Section 4108 of the Food and Agricultural Code.

(s) Employees of the Franchise Tax Board designated by the board, provided that the primary duty of these peace officers shall be the enforcement of the law as set forth in Chapter 9 (commencing with Section 19701) of Part 10.2 of Division

2 of the Revenue and Taxation Code.

(t) Notwithstanding any other provision of this section, a peace officer authorized by this section shall not be authorized to carry firearms by his or her employing agency until that agency has adopted a policy on the use of deadly force by those peace officers, and until those peace officers have been instructed in the employing agency's policy on the use of deadly force. Every peace officer authorized pursuant to this section to carry firearms by his or her employing agency shall qualify in the use of the firearms at least every six months.

(u) Investigators of the Department of Managed Health Care designated by the Director of the Department of Managed Health Care, provided that the primary duty of these investigators shall be the enforcement of the provisions of laws administered by the Director of the Department of Managed Health Care. Notwithstanding any other provision of law, the peace officers designated pursuant to this subdivision shall not carry firearms.

(v) The Chief, Deputy Chief, supervising investigators, and investigators of the Office of Protective Services of the State Department of Developmental Services, provided that the primary duty of each of those persons shall be the enforcement of the law relating to the duties of his or her department or office.

Probate Code

§ 4121. A power of attorney is legally sufficient if all of the following requirements are satisfied:

(a) The power of attorney contains the date of its execution.

(b) The power of attorney is signed either (1) by the principal or (2) in the principal's name by some other person in the principal's presence and at the principal's direction.

(c) The power of attorney is either (1) acknowledged before a notary public or (2) signed by at least two witnesses who satisfy the requirements of Section 4122.

§ 4122. If the power of attorney is signed by witnesses, as provided in Section 4121, the following requirements shall be satisfied:

(a) The witnesses shall be adults.

(b) The attorney-in-fact may not act as a witness.

(c) Each witness signing the power of attorney shall witness either the signing of the instrument by the principal or the principal's acknowledgment of the signature or the power of attorney.

(d) In the case of a durable power of attorney for health care, the additional requirements of Section 4701.

§ 4307. (a) A copy of a power of attorney certified under this section has the same force and effect as the original power of attorney.

(b) A copy of a power of attorney may be certified by any of the following:

(1) An attorney authorized to practice law in this state.

(2) A notary public in this state.

(3) An official of a state or of a political subdivision who is authorized to make certifications.

(c) The certification shall state that the certifying person has examined the original power of attorney and the copy and that the copy is a true and correct copy of the original power of attorney.

(d) Nothing in this section is intended to create an implication that a third person may be liable for acting in good faith reliance on a copy of a power of attorney that has not been certified under this section.

§ 4673. (a) A written advance health care directive is legally sufficient if all of the following requirements are satisfied:

(1) The advance directive contains the date of its execution.

(2) The advance directive is signed either by the patient or in the patient's name by another adult in the patient's presence and at the patient's direction.

(3) The advance directive is either acknowledged before a notary public or signed by at least two witnesses who satisfy the requirements of Sections 4674 and 4675.

(b) An electronic advance health care directive or power of attorney for health care is legally sufficient if the requirements in subdivision (a) are satisfied, except that for the purposes of paragraph (3) of subdivision (a), an acknowledgment before a notary public shall be required, and if a digital signature is used, it meets all of the following requirements:

(1) The digital signature either meets the requirements of Section 16.5 of the Government Code and Chapter 10 (commencing with Section 22000) of Division 7 of Title 2 of the California Code of Regulations or the digital signature uses an algorithm approved by the National Institute of Standards and Technology.

(2) The digital signature is unique to the person using it.

(3) The digital signature is capable of verification.

(4) The digital signature is under the sole control of the person using it.

(5) The digital signature is linked to data in such a manner that if the data are changed, the digital signature is invalidated.

(6) The digital signature persists with the document and not by association in separate files.

(7) The digital signature is bound to a digital certificate.

§ 4701. If the durable power of attorney for health care is signed by witnesses, as provided in Section 4121, in addition to the requirements applicable to witnesses under Section 4122, the following requirements shall be satisfied: ***

(e) If the principal is a patient in a skilled nursing facility, as defined in subdivision (c) of Section 1250 of the Health and Safety Code, at the time the durable power of attorney for health care is executed, the power of attorney is not effective unless a patient advocate or ombudsman as may be designated by the Department of Aging for this purpose pursuant to any other applicable provision of law signs the instrument as a witness, either as one of two witnesses or in addition to notarization pursuant to subdivision (c) of Section 4121. The patient advocate or ombudsman shall declare that he or she is serving as a witness as required by this subdivision. It is the intent of this subdivision to recognize that some patients in skilled nursing facilities are insulated from a voluntary decisionmaking role, by virtue of the custodial nature of their care, so as to require special assurance that they are capable of willfully and voluntarily executing a durable power of attorney for health care.

Health and Safety Code

§ 103526. (a) A faxed notary acknowledgment accompanying a faxed request received pursuant to this subdivision for a certified copy of a birth or death record or a military service record shall be legible and, if the notary's seal is not photographically reproducible, show the name of the notary, the county of the notary's principal place of business, the notary's telephone number, the notary's registration number, and the notary's commission expiration date typed or printed in a manner that is photographically reproducible below, or immediately adjacent to, the notary's signature in the acknowledgment.

Uniform Commercial Code

§ 3505.***

(b) A protest is a certificate of dishonor made by a United States consul or vice consul, or a notary public or other person authorized to administer oaths by the law of the place where dishonor occurs. It may be made upon information satisfactory to that person. The protest shall identify the instrument and certify either that presentment has been made or, if not made, the reason why it was not made, and that the instrument has been dishonored by nonacceptance or nonpayment. The protest may also certify that notice of dishonor has been given to some or all parties.

United States Code

§ 936. Art. 136. Authority to administer oaths and to act as notary

(a) The following persons on active duty or performing inactive-duty training may administer oaths for the purposes of military administration, including military justice:

(1) All judge advocates.

(2) All summary courts-martial.

(3) All adjutants, assistant adjutants, acting adjutants, and personnel adjutants.

(4) All commanding officers of the Navy, Marine Corps, and Coast Guard.

(5) All staff judge advocates and legal officers, and acting or assistant staff judge advocates and legal officers.

(6) All other persons designated by regulations of the armed forces or by statute.

(b) The following persons on active duty or performing inactive-duty training may administer oaths necessary in the performance of their duties:

(1) The president, military judge, trial counsel, and assistant trial counsel for all general and special courts-martial.

(2) The president and the counsel for the court of any court of inquiry.

(3) All officers designated to take a deposition.

(4) All persons detailed to conduct an investigation.

(5) All recruiting officers.

(6) All other persons designated by regulations of the armed forces or by statute.

§ 1044a. Authority to act as notary

(a) The persons named in subsection (b) have the general powers of a notary public and of a consul of the United States in the performance of all notarial acts to be executed by any of the following:

(1) Members of any of the armed forces.

(2) Other persons eligible for legal assistance under the provisions of section 1044 of this title or regulations of the Department of Defense.

(3) Persons serving with, employed by, or accompanying the armed forces outside the United States and outside the Commonwealth of Puerto Rico, Guam, and the Virgin Islands.

(4) Other persons subject to the Uniform Code of Military Justice (chapter 47

of this title) outside the United States.

(b) Persons with the powers described in subsection (a) are the following:

(1) All judge advocates, including reserve judge advocates when not in a duty status.

(2) All civilian attorneys serving as legal assistance attorneys.

(3) All adjutants, assistant adjutants, and personnel adjutants, including reserve members when not in a duty status.

(4) All other members of the armed forces, including reserve members when not in a duty status, who are designated by regulations of the armed forces or by statute to have those powers.

(5) For the performance of notarial acts at locations outside the United States, all employees of a military department or the Coast Guard who are designated by regulations of the Secretary concerned or by statute to have those powers for exercise outside the United States.

(c) No fee may be paid to or received by any person for the performance of a notarial act authorized in this section.

(d) The signature of any such person acting as notary, together with the title of that person's offices, is prima facie evidence that the signature is genuine, that the person holds the designated title, and that the person is authorized to perform a notarial act. ■

Offices of the California Secretary of State

Sacramento

Mailing Address:
Secretary of State
Notary Public Section
P.O. Box 942877
Sacramento, CA 94277-0001
Telephone: (916) 653-3595
Web site: www.sos.ca.gov

Street Address:
Secretary of State
Notary Public Section
1500 11th St., 2nd Floor
Sacramento, CA 95814

Los Angeles

Los Angeles Office
Secretary of State
300 South Spring Street
12th Floor, South Tower,
Suite 12513
Los Angeles, CA 90013
(213) 897-3062

San Diego

San Diego Office
Secretary of State
1350 Front Street, Suite 2060
San Diego, CA 92101
(619) 525-4113

County Clerks' Offices

Upon receiving a new commission, the Notary must file an oath of office and bond with the county clerk's office in the county of the Notary's principal place of business. The oath and bond must be filed within 30 days of the commission starting date.

At these same offices, certificates authenticating a local Notary's signature and seal may be obtained by anyone presenting a document notarized by the particular local Notary.

For certified copies of marriage certificates, contact the office of the county clerk where the certificate was filed.

Alameda County
1106 Madison St., Rm. 101
Oakland 94607
(510) 272-6362

Alpine County
P.O. Box 158
99 Water St.
Markleeville 96120
(530) 694-2281

Amador County
500 Argonaut Lane
Jackson 95642-0953
(209) 223-6468

Butte County
25 County Center Dr.
Oroville 95965
(530) 538-7761

Calaveras County
891 Mountain Ranch Rd.
San Andreas 95249
(209) 754-6371

Colusa County
Courthouse
546 Jay St.
Colusa 95932
(530) 458-0500

Contra Costa County
P.O. Box 350
822 Main St.
Martinez 94553
(925) 646-2360

Del Norte County
981 H St., Suite 160
Crescent City 95531
(707) 464-7216

El Dorado County
360 Fair Lane
Placerville 95667
(530) 621-5490

3368 Lake Tahoe Blvd.
Suite 108
S. Lake Tahoe 96150
(530) 573-3408

Fresno County
2221 Kern St.
Fresno 93721
(559) 488-3003

Glenn County
P.O. Box 391
Willows 95988
(530) 934-6400

Humboldt County
825 Fifth St., 5th Floor
Eureka 95501-1172
(707) 445-7593

Imperial County
940 Main St., #202
El Centro 92243-2839
(760) 482-4226

Inyo County
P.O. Box F
168 N. Edwards St.
Independence 93526
(760) 878-9223

Kern County
1115 Truxtun Ave.
Bakersfield 93301
(661) 868-3599

Kings County
1400 W. Lacey Blvd.
Hanford 93230
(559) 582-3211 ext. 2486

Lake County
255 N. Forbes St.
Lakeport 95453
(707) 263-2311

Lassen County
Courthouse
220 S. Lassen St., #5
Susanville 96130
(530) 251-8217

Los Angeles County
*Mailing address for all
L.A. County:*
Business Filing &
Registration
12400 E. Imperial Hwy.,
Second Floor, Rm. 2001
Norwalk 90650
(562) 462-2177

*Walk-in addresses
(does not accept mail):*
335A East Avenue K-6
Lancaster 93535
(661) 723-4494

12400 E. Imperial Hwy.,
#2001
Norwalk 90650
(562) 462-2177

14340 Sylvan St.
Van Nuys 91401
(818) 374-7192

11701 S. La Cienega Bl.
6th Floor
Los Angeles 90045
(310) 727-6142

Madera County
209 W. Yosemite Ave.
Madera 93637
(559) 675-7720

Marin County
P.O. Box E
San Rafael 94913
(415) 499-6415

Mariposa County
P.O. Box 247
4982 10th St.
Mariposa 95338-0247
(209) 966-2007

Mendocino County
501 Low Gap Rd., #1020
Ukiah 95482
(707) 463-4370

Merced County
2222 M St., Rm. 14
Merced 95340
(209) 385-7501

Modoc County
204 Court St.
Alturas 96101
(530) 233-6201

Mono County
P.O. Box 696
Bridgeport 93517
(760) 932-5241

Monterey County
P.O. Box 29
240 Church St., Rm. 305
Salinas 93902
(831) 755-5041

Napa County
900 Coombs, Rm. 116
Napa 94559
(707) 253-4246

Nevada County
950 Maidu Ave.
Nevada City 95959
(530) 265-1221

Orange County
P.O. Box 238
12 Civic Center Plaza,
Room 106
Santa Ana 92702
(714) 834-2500

Placer County
2954 Richardson Dr.
Auburn 95603
(530) 886-5600

Plumas County
520 Main St., Rm. 102
Quincy 95971
(530) 283-6218

Riverside County
P.O. Box 751
2720 & 2724 Gateway Dr.
Riverside 92507
(909) 486-7000

880 N. State St., Ste. B-6
Hemet 92543-1496
(909) 766-2500

**County Administrative
Center**
82-675 Hwy. 111, Rm. 113
Indio 92201-5994
(760) 863-8732

*Walk-in addresses
(does not accept mail):*
4080 Lemon St., 1st Fl.
Riverside 92502-2204
(909) 486-7000

**County Administrative
Center**
270 N. Broadway
Blythe 92225-1608
(760) 921-7981

Sacramento County
P.O. Box 839
600 8th Street
Sacramento 95812-0839
(916) 874-6334
(800) 313-7133

San Benito County
440 5th St., #206
Hollister 95023-3843
(831) 636-4029

**San Bernardino
County**
222 W. Hospitality Ln.
San Bernardino
92415-0022
(909) 386-8970

San Diego County
1600 Pacific Hwy., #260
San Diego 92101
(619) 237-0502

334 Via Vera Cruz, #150
San Marcos 92069
(760) 940-6868

9225 Clairemont Mesa Bl.
San Diego 92123
(858) 505-6262

590 Third Avenue
Chula Vista 91910
(619) 498-2200

200 S. Magnolia Ave.
El Cajon 92020
(619) 401-5700

San Francisco County
City Hall Rm. 168
1 Dr. Carlton B.
Goodlet Pl.
San Francisco
94102-4678
(415) 554-4950

San Joaquin County
Pacific State Bank Bldg.
6 S. El Dorado St., 2nd Fl.
Stockton 95202
(209) 468-3939

San Luis Obispo County
1144 Monterey St.
San Luis Obispo 93408
(805) 781-5080

5955 Capistrano, Suite B
Hotel Park Business
Park
Atascadero 93422
(805) 461-6041

San Mateo County
555 County Center, 1st Fl.
Redwood City 94063
(650) 363-4212

Santa Barbara County
P.O. Box 159
1100 Anacapa St.
Santa Barbara
93102-0159
(805) 568-2250

Walk-in address
(does not accept mail):
511 E. Lakeside Pkwy.
Santa Maria 93455-1341
(805) 346-8370

401 E. Cypress Ave.,
#102
Lompoc 93436
(805) 737-7705

Santa Clara County
70 W. Hedding Street
1st Floor, East Wing
San Jose 95110
(408) 299-5665

Santa Cruz County
701 Ocean St., #230
Santa Cruz 95060
(831) 454-2470

Shasta County
P.O. Box 990880
1643 Market St.
Redding 96099-0880
(530) 225-5730

Sierra County
100 Courthouse Square
P.O. Box D
Downieville 95936-0938
(530) 289-3295

Siskiyou County
311 4th Street, Room 201
Yreka 96097
(530) 842-8084

Solano County
600 Texas St.
Fairfield 94533
(707) 421-7510

Sonoma County
2300 County Center Dr.,
Ste. B177
Santa Rosa 95403
(707) 565-3800

Stanislaus County
1021 I St., Ste. 101
Modesto 95354
(209) 525-5250

Sutter County
P.O. Box 1555
433 Second St.
Yuba City 95991
(530) 822-7134

Tehama County
P.O. Box 250
633 Washington St. #11
Red Bluff 96080
(530) 527-3350

Trinity County
P.O. Box 1258
101 Court St.
Weaverville 96093
(530) 623-1220

Tulare County
221 S. Mooney Blvd.
#105
Visalia 93291-4593
(559) 733-6418

Tuolumne County
2 S. Green St.
Sonora 95370
(209) 533-5570

Ventura County
800 S. Victoria Avenue
Ventura 93009-1200
(805) 654-2264/2666

Yolo County
625 Court St., Rm. 105
P.O. Box 1130
Woodland 95695
(530) 666-8130

Yuba County
935 14th St.
Marysville 95910
(530) 741-6341

Bureaus of Vital Statistics

California Notaries are not permitted to make certified copies of any document except powers of attorney and entries in their journals. Persons requesting notarization or certified copies of birth or death certificates should be referred to the respective state public office (below) that can provide certified copies of vital records. Persons requiring copies of foreign records should contact the appropriate consulate in the United States.

New criteria for a notarized request for a certified copy of birth or death records in California are outlined in the Health and Safety Code, Section 103526(a). (See page 128.)

Alabama
Vital Records
Department of Public Health
P.O. Box 5625
Montgomery, AL 36103-5625

Alaska
Bureau of Vital Statistics
Dept. of Health & Social Services
5441 Commercial Blvd.
P.O. Box 110675
Juneau, AK 99801

Arizona
Office of Vital Records
Department of Health Services
P.O. Box 3887
Phoenix, AZ 85030-3887

Arkansas
Division of Vital Records
Department of Health
4815 West Markham St., Slot 44
Little Rock, AR 72205-3867

California
Office of Vital Records
Department of Health Services
P.O. Box 997410, MS: 5103
Sacramento, CA 95899-7410

Colorado
Vital Records Section
Department of Health
4300 Cherry Creek Drive South
Denver, CO 80246-1530

Connecticut
Connecticut Department of
Public Health
State Office of Vital Records
410 Capitol Ave., MS#11VRS
P.O. Box 340308
Hartford, CT 06134-0308

Delaware
Delaware Health Statistics Center
Office of Vital Statistics
Jesse S. Cooper Building
417 Federal Street
Dover, DE 19901

District of Columbia
Vital Records Division
825 North Capitol St. NE,
1st Floor
Washington, DC 20002

Florida
Office of Vital Statistics
1217 Pearl Street
P.O. Box 210
Jacksonville, FL 32231

Georgia
Vital Records
2600 Skyland Drive NE
Atlanta, GA 30319-3640

Hawaii
Vital Statistics Section
State Department of Health
P.O. Box 3378
Honolulu, HI 96801

Idaho
Vital Statistics Unit
450 West State Street, 1st Floor
P.O. Box 83720
Boise, ID 83720-0036

Illinois
Division of Vital Records
Department of Public Health
605 West Jefferson Street
Springfield, IL 62702-5097

Indiana
Vital Records Department
Indiana State Department of Health
6 West Washington Street
Indianapolis, IN 46204

Iowa
Department of Public Health
Bureau of Vital Records
Lucas Office Building, 1st Floor
321 East 12th Street
Des Moines, IA 50319-0075

Kansas
Office of Vital Statistics
1000 SW Jackson Street,
Suite 120
Topeka, KS 66612-2221

Kentucky
Office of Vital Statistics
Department for Health Services
275 East Main Street, 1E-A
Frankfort, KY 40621-0001

Louisiana
Vital Records Registry
P.O. Box 60630
New Orleans, LA 70160

Maine
Vital Statistics
221 State Street
11 State House Station
Augusta, ME 04333-0011

Maryland
Division of Vital Records
Department of Health
6550 Reisterstown Road
Baltimore, MD 21215

Massachusetts
Registry of Vital Records
and Statistics
150 Mount Vernon St., 1st Floor
Dorchester, MA 02125-3105

Michigan
Vital Records Request
P.O. Box 30721
Lansing, MI 48909

Minnesota
Minnesota Department of Health
Attention: Office of the
State Registrar
P.O. Box 64882
St. Paul, MN 55164-0882

Mississippi
Vital Records
P.O. Box 1700
Jackson, MS 39215-1700

Missouri
Department of Health
Bureau of Vital Records
930 Wildwood
P.O. Box 570
Jefferson City, MO 65102-0570

Montana
Office of Vital Statistics
P.O. Box 4210
111 North Sanders, Room 209
Helena, MT 59604

Nebraska
Vital Statistics
Department of Health
301 Centennial Mall South
P.O. Box 95065
Lincoln, NE 68509-5065

Nevada
Office of Vital Records
4150 Technology Way, Suite 104
Carson City, NV 89706

New Hampshire
New Hampshire Department
of State
Division of Vital Records
Administration
71 South Fruit Street
Concord, NH 03301-2410

New Jersey
Vital Statistics
Customer Service
P.O. Box 370
Trenton, NJ 08625-0370

New Mexico
Vital Records
1105 St. Francis Drive
Santa Fe, NM 87502

New York
New York State Department of
Health
Vital Records Section
Certification Unit
P.O. Box 2602
Albany, NY 12220-2602

New York City
Office of Vital Records
New York City Dept. of Health
125 Worth St., CN4, Room 133
New York, NY 10013

North Carolina
Vital Records
1903 Mail Service Center
Raleigh, NC 27699-1903

North Dakota
Division of Vital Records
600 E. Boulevard Ave., Dept. 301
Bismarck, ND 58505-0200

Ohio
Ohio Department of Health
Vital Statistics
P.O. Box 15098
Columbus, OH 43215-0098

Oklahoma
Vital Records Service
State Department of Health
1000 Northeast 10th Street
Oklahoma City, OK 73117

Oregon
Vital Records
P.O. Box 14050
Portland, OR 97293-0050

Pennsylvania
Division of Vital Records
101 South Mercer St., Room 401
P.O. Box 1528
New Castle, PA 16101

Rhode Island
Office of Vital Records
Department of Health
3 Capitol Hill Rd., Room 101
Providence, RI 02908-5097

South Carolina
Office of Vital Records
South Carolina DHEC
2600 Bull Street
Columbia, SC 29201

South Dakota
Vital Records
207 E. Missouri Ave., Suite #1A
Pierre, SD 57501

Tennessee
Vital Records
Central Services Building
421 5th Avenue North
Nashville, TN 37247

Texas
Bureau of Vital Statistics
Department of Health
P.O. Box 12040
Austin, TX 78711-2040

Utah
Vital Records & Statistics
Cannon Health Building
288 North 1460 West
P.O. Box 141012
Salt Lake City, UT 84114-1012

Vermont
Department of Health
Vital Records Section
108 Cherry Street
P.O. Box 70
Burlington, VT 05402-0070

Virginia
Office of Vital Records
P.O. Box 1000
Richmond, VA 23218-1000

Washington
Department of Health
Center for Health Statistics
P.O. Box 9709
Olympia, WA 98507-9709

West Virginia
Vital Registration Office
350 Capitol Street, Room 165
Charleston, WV 25301-3701

Wisconsin
Vital Records
1 West Wilson Street
P.O. Box 309
Madison, WI 53701-0309

Wyoming
Vital Records Services
Hathaway Building
Cheyenne, WY 82002

American Samoa
LBJ Tropical Medical Center
Department of Health Services
American Samoa Government
Pago Pago, AS 96799

Guam
Office of Vital Statistics
Department of Public Health
P.O. Box 2816
Agana, GU, M.I. 96910

Northern Mariana Islands
Bureau of Health Planning
Vital Statistics Office
P.O. Box 500409 CK
Saipan, MP 96950-0409

Panama Canal Zone
Vital Records Section
Passport Services
U.S. Department of State
1111 19th Street NW, Suite 510
Washington, DC 20522-1705

Puerto Rico
Department of Health
Demographic Registry
P.O. Box 11854
Fernández Juncos Station
San Juan, PR 00910

Virgin Islands (St. Croix)
Department of Health
Vital Statistics
Charles Harwood Memorial Hospital
St. Croix, VI 00820

**Virgin Islands
(St. Thomas, St. John)**
Department of Health
Registrar of Vital Statistics
Knud Hansen Complex
St. Thomas, VI 00802

Hague Convention Nations

The nations listed on the following pages are parties to a treaty called the *Hague Convention Abolishing the Requirement of Legalization (Authentication) for Foreign Public Documents.*

Treaty Simplifies Authentication. A Notary's signature on documents that are sent to these nations may be authenticated (verified as valid for the benefit of the recipient in the foreign nation) by California's Secretary of State through attachment of a single certificate of authenticity called an *apostille*. The *apostille* (French for "notation") is the only authentication certificate necessary. Nations not subscribing to the Hague Convention may require as many as five or six separate authenticating certificates from different governmental agencies, domestic and foreign.

How to Request an *Apostille.* To obtain an apostille, anyone may mail the notarized document and a $20 check payable to the "Secretary of State" to:

> Office of Secretary of State
> Notary Public Section
> P.O. Box 942877
> Sacramento, CA 94277-0001

An apostille must be specifically requested, and the nation to which the document will be sent must be indicated. In person, an apostille may be obtained at 1500 11th Street, 2nd Floor, in Sacramento, but the cost for an in-person request is $26.

It is not the Notary's responsibility to obtain an *apostille*; it is the responsibility of the party needing authentication.

Hague Convention Nations. The following nations participate in the Hague Convention:

Albania
Andorra[10]
Antigua and
    Barbuda[10]
Argentina[1]
Armenia[10]
Australia
Austria
Azerbaijan
Bahamas[10]
Barbados[10]
Belarus
Belgium
Belize[10]
Bosnia-
    Herzegovina[2]
Botswana[10]
Brunei
    Darussalam[10]
Bulgaria
Colombia[10]
Cook Islands

Croatia[2]
Cyprus
Czech Republic
Denmark
Dominica[10]
Ecuador
El Salvador[10]
Estonia
Fiji[10]
Finland
France[3]
Georgia
Germany
Greece
Grenada[10]
Honduras[10]
Hong Kong[4]
Hungary
Iceland
India
Ireland
Israel

Italy
Japan
Kazakhstan[10]
Latvia
Lesotho[10]
Liberia[5and10]
Liechtenstein[10]
Lithuania
Luxembourg
Macao[4]
Macedonia[2]
Malawi[10]
Malta
Marshall
    Islands[10]
Mauritius[10]
Mexico
Moldova
Monaco
Montenegro[2]
Namibia[10]
Netherlands[6]

1. Excludes recognition of extension of the Convention by the United Kingdom to the Malvinas (Falkland Islands), South Georgia, South Sandwich Islands and the Argentine Antarctic Sector.

2. The former Yugoslavia was a party to the Convention. Only the breakaway nations of Bosnia-Herzegovina, Croatia, Macedonia, Montenegro, Serbia and Slovenia have confirmed that the Convention still applies.

3. This nation includes Comoros Islands, Djibouti, French Guyana, French Polynesia, Guadeloupe, Martinique, New Caledonia, Reunion, St. Pierre and Miquelon, and Wallis and Futuna. (Names appearing in regular type denote territories; *italic type denotes now-independent nations that have not affirmed participation in the Convention.*)

4. This nation retained its status as a Hague nation after control was returned to China on July 1, 1997 (Hong Kong) and December 20, 1999 (Macao).

5. The Convention does not apply between Liberia and the United States.

10. This nation is not a member of the *Hague Conference on Private International Law* but has signed the *Hague Convention Abolishing the Requirement of Legalization for Foreign Public Documents.*

New Zealand
Niue[10]
North Korea
Norway
Panama
Poland
Portuga[17]
Romania
Russian
    Federation
Saint Kitts and
    Nevis[10]
Saint Lucia[10]

Saint Vincent
    and the
    Grenadines[10]
Samoa[10]
San Marino[10]
São Tomé e
    Principe
Serbia
Seychelles[10]
Slovakia
Slovenia[2]
South Africa
Spain

Suriname
Swaziland[10]
Sweden
Switzerland
Tonga[10]
Trinidad and
    Tobago[10]
Turkey
Ukraine
United
    Kingdom[8]
United States[5and9]
Venezuela

Inquiries. Persons having questions about the *Hague Convention Abolishing the Requirement of Legalization for Foreign Public Documents* may address their inquiries to:

Authentication Office
518 23rd Street, N.W.
State Annex 1
Washington, DC 20037
(202) 647-5002

---

2. The former Yugoslavia was a party to the Convention. Only the breakaway nations of Bosnia-Herzegovina, Croatia, Macedonia, Serbia and Montenegro and Slovenia have confirmed that the Convention still applies.

6. Extended to all Aruba, Curacao and Netherlands Antilles.

7. Extended to Angola, Mozambique and all overseas territories.

8. United Kingdom of Great Britain and Northern Ireland is extended to Anguilla, Bermuda, British Antarctica Territory, British Virgin Islands, Cayman Islands, Falkland Islands, Gibraltar, Guyana, Guernsey, Isle of Man, Jersey, Kiribati, Montserrat, St. Helena, Solomon Islands, Turks and Caicos Islands, Tuvalu, Vanuatu and Zimbabwe. (Names appearing in regular type denote territories; *italic type denotes now-independent nations that have not affirmed participation in the Convention.*)

9. This nation includes American Samoa, District of Columbia, Guam, Northern Mariana Islands, Puerto Rico and U.S. Virgin Islands.

10. This nation is not a member of the *Hague Conference on Private International Law* but has signed the *Hague Convention Abolishing the Requirement of Legalization for Foreign Public Documents.* ■

About
the NNA

Since 1957, the National Notary Association — a nonprofit educational organization — has served the nation's Notaries Public with a wide variety of instructional programs and services.

As the country's clearinghouse for information on notarial laws, customs and practices, the NNA educates Notaries through publications, seminars, annual conferences and a Notary Information Service that offers immediate answers to specific questions about notarization.

The Association is perhaps most widely known as the preeminent source of information for and about Notaries. NNA works include:

- *The National Notary*, a magazine for National Notary Association members featuring how-to articles and practical tips on notarizing.

- *Notary Bulletin,* an eNewsletter that keeps NNA members up to date on developments affecting Notaries, especially new state laws and regulations.

- *Notary Basics Made Easy*, a first-of-its-kind video instruction program that simplifies Notary practices and procedures.

- *Notary Home Study Course*, a work-at-your-own-speed course covering every facet of notarization.

- *Sorry, No Can Do!* series, four volumes that help Notaries explain to customers and bosses why some requests for notarizations are improper and cannot be accommodated.

- *U.S. Notary Reference Manual*, an invaluable resource for any person relying upon the authenticity and correctness of legal documents.

- *Notary Public Practices & Glossary*, widely hailed as the Notary's bible, a definitive reference book on notarial procedures.

- State *Notary Law Primers*, short guide books that explain a state's notarial statutes in easy-to-understand language.

- *The Model Notary Act*, prototype legislation conceived in 1973 and updated in 1984 and 2002 by an NNA-recruited panel of secretaries of state, legislators and attorneys, and regularly used by state legislatures in revising their notarial laws.

- *Notary Law & Practice: Cases & Materials*, the definitive and one-of-a-kind text for teaching Notary law to law students in schools and to attorneys in Minimum Continuing Education Seminars (MCLE), discussing every major judicial decision affecting the Notary's duties.

- *Notary Signing Agent Certification Course*, an invaluable resource for candidates preparing to complete the Notary Signing Agent Certification Examination developed by the National Notary Association.

- Public-service pamphlets informing the general public about the function of a Notary, including *What Is A Notary Public?*, printed in English and Spanish.

In addition, the National Notary Association offers the highest quality professional supplies, including official seals and stamps, embossers, recordkeeping journals, affidavit stamps, thumbprinting devices and notarial certificates.

Though dedicated primarily to educating and assisting Notaries, the National Notary Association devotes part of its resources to helping lawmakers draft effective notarial statutes and to informing the public about the Notary's vital role in modern society. ■

Index

Page numbers listed in **bold** indicate where the most complete information on a subject can be found. *Italics* indicate the pages where the statutes pertaining to a subject are located.

Page numbers listed in **bold** indicate where the most complete information on a subject can be found. *Italics* indicate the pages where the statutes pertaining to a subject are located.

Page numbers listed in **bold** indicate where the most complete information on a subject can be found. *Italics* indicate the pages where the statutes pertaining to a subject are located.

Page numbers listed in **bold** indicate where the most complete information on a
subject can be found. *Italics* indicate the pages where the statutes pertaining to a
subject are located.

Page numbers listed in **bold** indicate where the most complete information on a subject can be found. *Italics* indicate the pages where the statutes pertaining to a subject are located.

Page numbers listed in **bold** indicate where the most complete information on a subject can be found. *Italics* indicate the pages where the statutes pertaining to a subject are located.